AS/A-LEVEL
UK Government and Politics

A. J. Turner

ESSENTIAL WORD
DICTIONARY

To Jo

Philip Allan Updates
Market Place
Deddington
Oxfordshire
OX15 0SE

Tel: 01869 338652
Fax: 01869 337590
e-mail: sales@philipallan.co.uk
www.philipallan.co.uk

ISBN 0 86003 381 3

Printed by Raithby, Lawrence & Co Ltd, Leicester

P00023

Introduction

a dictionary of words and phrases used in the AS and A2 modules in ...evel specifications on the government and politics of the United Kingdom. For this reason, the definitions are in some cases broader and in others narrower than they would be for the ordinary usage of these words and phrases. The dictionary is not intended as a substitute for a textbook but the definitions are developed, in short accompanying paragraphs, to give further explanations and useful examples. The most up-to-date and pertinent examples at the time of writing have been included although, due to the nature of the subject, many of these will be superseded. Also included are a number of tips to highlight common misunderstandings, comparisons with other political systems and additional points of interest. Throughout the dictionary there are italicised cross-references to words and phrases defined elsewhere which contribute to a more complete understanding of an entry's meaning.

Acknowledgements

Thanks are due to my wife, Jo, for substituting sleep and reading for pleasure on her train journeys to work with reading and correcting early drafts of this dictionary, to my father for his research and to Eric Magee for his helpful comments and suggestions. Finally, I would like to acknowledge the contribution made by Ariadne Birnberg who once asked how I spent my outrageously long holidays.

AJT

accountability: the requirement that public office-holders (particularly those who receive a salary from public funds) are answerable to the public regarding their duties and responsibilities.

■ **e.g.** A government *minister* is regarded as being publicly accountable through *parliament* and an MP is considered accountable to the voters in his/her *constituency*.

active citizenship: an idea associated with Conservative governments of the 1980s and 1990s which emphasised the responsibilities of *citizens* and discouraged reliance on the *state*.

● Active citizenship found expression in voluntary work, Neighbourhood Watch schemes and, most notably, the *Citizen's Charter*.

activist: someone who is actively involved in the political process, usually through membership of a *political party* or *pressure group*.

act of parliament: a law created as the result of a *bill* completing its passage through *parliament*.

● Also known as a *statute*, it achieves its status as a law by being voted through the *House of Commons* and the *House of Lords* and receiving the *Royal Assent*.

● An act is the result of a bill completing a series of steps known as the *legislative process*.

Adam Smith Institute: a *right-wing think-tank* founded in the USA in 1978 and established in the UK in 1981.

● This think-tank, named after the eighteenth-century philosopher and economist, was particularly influential in the 1980s. *Margaret Thatcher*'s Conservative governments adopted its *neo-liberal* or *New Right* ideas on *privatisation*.

additional member system (AMS): a *hybrid electoral system* in which members of a *legislature* are elected in one of two ways: some by *simple plurality* in *single-member constituencies* and others through regional *party lists* to ensure a degree of *proportionality*.

● The additional members elected through party lists are allocated using the *d'Hondt Formula*.

■ **e.g.** Germany and New Zealand use AMS. Versions of this system are also used for elections to the *Scottish Parliament* and *Welsh Assembly*.

adjournment debate: a *debate* on an issue of personal or *constituency* interest raised by a *backbench MP* in the final half hour of a day's sitting in the *House of Commons*.

adversarial politics: antagonistic competition between the two main *political parties* at *Westminster* offering to implement contrasting programmes in government.

- The theory, associated with Professor S. E. Finer, was used particularly to describe politics in the UK in the 1970s.
- *TIP* Contrast adverserial politics with *consensus politics* in the 1950s and following the fall of *Margaret Thatcher* in the 1990s.

adviser (political or special adviser): a political appointee — rather than a career *civil servant* — employed by a government *minister*. See also *spin doctor*.

- There has been an increased number of political advisers in *Whitehall* since *Margaret Thatcher*'s premiership (and particularly under *Tony Blair*) which has fuelled criticism of the politicisation of the civil service.
- *e.g. Chancellor of the exchequer* Nigel Lawson cited Thatcher's preference for consultation with her economics adviser Professor Sir Alan Walters as the reason for his resignation from the *cabinet* in 1989.

affiliated: the adjective describing a group or individual linked or associated with a *political party*.

- The *Labour Party* has a number of affiliated organisations that play a part in its internal procedures. Many *trade union* members are entitled to become affiliated members of the party as a result of paying the *political levy*. This allows them to participate in policy-making and leadership elections.
- *e.g.* The Transport and General Workers' Union and the *Fabian Society* are affiliated to the Labour Party.
- *TIP* The voting power of the affiliated members (who are more numerous than ordinary members) has long been a contentious issue in the Labour Party.

agency: see *executive agency*.

alignment: the long-term and consistent inclination to vote for a particular *political party* observed in the *electorate*.

- The term is used to describe the situation in which a voter or group of voters can be relied upon to vote for the same party from election to election.
- *e.g.* Both *class* and *partisan alignment* were significant features of *voting behaviour* in the UK from 1945 until the 1970s, after which *dealignment* was observed.
- *TIP* Take care to distinguish between class and partisan alignment, but note that they are related.

alternative vote (AV): an *electoral system* which elects *candidates* in *single-member constituencies* and in which the voter is invited to rank the candidates on the *ballot paper* in order of preference.

- The winning candidate is the one who secures more than 50% of the votes. If no candidate secures more than 50% of first preference votes, the bottom candidate is eliminated and his or her second preference votes are allocated to the remaining candidates. This process continues until a candidate reaches more than 50% of the votes cast.

■ *e.g.* This system is used for elections to the House of Representatives in Australia.

■ *TIP* AV does not produce proportional results. Take care to distinguish between *majoritarian electoral systems*, such as this one, and *proportional electoral systems*.

amendment: a change made to a *bill* permitted at certain stages of the *legislative process*.

● The government's control of the legislative process enables it to introduce amendments to bills during their passage into legislation. *Opposition parties* and individual MPs are rarely able to introduce amendments without government support.

AMS: see *additional member system*.

Amsterdam, Treaty of (1997): the treaty between *European Union member states* that gave the *European Parliament* a greater role in decision-making and a potential *veto* over legislative proposals from the *Council of Ministers*.

● The Treaty of Amsterdam also extended *qualified majority voting* to 11 new policy areas.

annual conference: see *conference*.

Ashdown, Paddy (1941–): the former *Liberal Democrat* MP for Yeovil (elected in 1983 as a *Liberal Party* MP) and leader of the Liberal Democrat Party from 1989 to 1999.

● Ashdown was responsible for forging closer relations with the *Labour Party* and secured seats on the *Joint Cabinet Committee on Constitutional Reform* in the Labour government after 1997.

authority: the right to govern (or be obeyed) which, in a *democracy,* is granted by the people and limited by certain laws, particularly the *constitution*.

■ *e.g.* The UK *Parliament* has the authority to pass *legislation* to levy taxes.

AV: see *alternative vote*.

AV plus: the *hybrid electoral system* recommended in the 1998 *Jenkins Report*.

● Under this system MPs would be elected in one of two ways. Most would be elected in *single-member constituencies* using the *alternative vote* and, to ensure greater *proportionality* than at present, a minority of top-up MPs (between 15 and 20% of the total) would be elected from regional open party lists of candidates. The voter would cast two votes on the *ballot paper*, one constituency and one list vote.

backbencher/backbench MP: a *Member of Parliament*, either on the *government* or *opposition* side, who does not have responsibilities as a major spokesperson for his or her *political party* (as a member of the *front bench*).

- The term comes from the position of the seats occupied by such MPs in the *House of Commons*.

backbench rebellion (or revolt): see *rebellion*.

ballot bill: type of *Private Member's Bill* which MPs have the right to introduce if their name is one of the 20 drawn at random from those wishing to promote *legislation* at the start of each *parliamentary session*.

- Largely due to the lack of time set aside to debate such bills (12 Fridays in each parliamentary session), only the top six MPs of the 20 drawn in the ballot stand a realistic chance of having their bills properly debated. Most of these still fail.

ballot box: a secure container where *voters* deposit *ballot papers* once they have recorded their *votes*.

- The box ensures the security and secrecy of the votes until they are counted and the results announced.

ballot paper: the piece of paper issued at a *polling station* on which a *voter* records a *vote* in *elections*.

- *Spoilt ballot* papers are those that do not count for a *candidate* because the vote has not been recorded in the correct manner and the intention of the voter is therefore unclear.

bandwagon effect: a disputed theory that a *political party* which is ahead in *opinion polls* will, as the most popular, attract the votes of those wishing to back the favourite and thereby increase the party's lead. See also *boomerang effect*.

bicameral legislature: a legislative body comprising two chambers or houses, such as the UK *Parliament* with the *Houses of Commons* and *Lords*. See also *unicameral legislature*.

- An advantage of a bicameral legislature is that the chambers are able to scrutinise each other's work.

- **e.g.** The US Congress' Senate and House of Representatives is a further example of a bicameral legislature.

bill: a proposed law before *parliament* that may or may not complete its passage into approved *legislation* and become a *statute*. See also *Private Member's Bill*.

● The government sponsors most bills (see *public bill* and *private bill*).

bipartisan: the adjective describing cooperation between the two main *political parties*.

▨ *e.g.* The *Conservative* and *Labour Parties* have largely adopted a bipartisan approach to the peace process in Northern Ireland, both supporting the *Good Friday Agreement*.

Blair, Tony (1953–): The Labour MP for Sedgefield, leader of the *Labour Party* since 1994 and *prime minister* since 1997.

● Blair continued the internal reforms of the Labour Party, begun by previous leaders *Neil Kinnock* and *John Smith*. These were designed to democratise the party, distance it from the *trade unions* and make it more attractive to the *electorate*. He is associated with the *Third Way* political *ideology*.

● Blair led the Labour Party to its biggest ever *general election* victory in 1997 and in the 2001 general election it won re-election and a full second term for the first time in the party's history.

● As prime minister, Blair has been responsible for a programme of *constitutional reform*. He has been criticised for his *presidential* style of leadership.

block vote: the former *Labour Party* practice that enabled *affiliated* organisations to cast an entitlement of votes based on the number of members they represented.

● The vote was cast as a single block, without the affiliated organisation necessarily consulting its members to ascertain their preferences.

● The block vote applied at the party *conference*, in leadership elections and in the selection of *parliamentary candidates*.

● In theory, the block vote should have disappeared with the introduction of *one member, one vote* in 1993 but, in practice, it may still be observed. For example, block votes were cast in the *electoral college* used for the selection of the Labour Party candidate for the London mayoral election and, at conference, block votes may still be used as consultation with members is often impractical.

▨ *TIP* The block vote is regarded as undemocratic and is associated with *Old Labour* and the former power of *trade union* leaders within the Labour Party.

BNP: see *British National Party*.

boomerang effect: a disputed theory that a *political party* which is trailing in *opinion polls* will, as the underdog, attract sympathy votes and thereby reduce the other party's lead. See also *bandwagon effect*.

● The boomerang effect can also result from complacency amongst supporters of the leading party, resulting in their failure to vote.

borough council: one of 33 elected *local government* assemblies in London.

▨ *e.g.* Hackney Borough Council.

Boundary Commissions: permanent independent bodies (one each for England, Scotland, Wales and Northern Ireland), chaired by the *speaker* of the *House of*

Commons, responsible for locating the boundaries of parliamentary *constituencies*. See also *gerrymandering*.

- At intervals of between 10 and 15 years, the commissions review constituency boundaries and recommend changes with the aim of maintaining constituencies containing approximately the same number of voters.

Bow Group: the liberal conservative faction within the *Conservative Party*, established in 1951.

British National Party (BNP): *far-right* fringe party, with strongly *nationalist* views particularly on immigration, which fields *candidates* at elections but attracts limited support in terms of votes.

- In the 2001 *general election*, local racial tension resulted in the BNP polling exceptionally high numbers of votes in the Oldham and Saddleworth, and Oldham West and Royton, *constituencies* (11% and 16% respectively).

broadsheet: a type of newspaper printed on A2-size paper and associated with more serious and detailed political analysis. See also *tabloid*.

▓ *e.g.* **The Times**, the **Daily Telegraph**, the **Guardian** and the **Independent**.

Bruges Group: faction within the *Conservative Party*, established after *Margaret Thatcher*'s euro-sceptic speech at Bruges in 1988 to oppose moves towards further *integration* in Europe.

Budget: the *chancellor of the exchequer's* annual statement containing plans for government spending and taxation, presented to *parliament* for passage into *legislation*.

- The Budget is the most important and high-profile piece of legislation presented to parliament each year.

▓ *TIP* Governments often use the Budget introduced immediately before a *general election* to cut taxation and increase public spending. The 2001 Budget, for example, was regarded by some as an attempt to win votes.

by-election: an *election* between *general elections* — usually held due to a vacancy arising as the result of the death or resignation of the sitting MP — at which a single *constituency* elects its MP for the *House of Commons*.

▓ *e.g.* In 1999 a by-election was held in Kensington and Chelsea following the death of the sitting MP, Alan Clark, and in 2000 a by-election was held in West Bromwich West when Betty Boothroyd retired as the constituency's MP. Unusually, a disputed 1997 general election result in Winchester prompted the High Court to rule that a by-election be held because a number of *ballot papers* crucial to the result had not been counted.

cabinet: the government committee chaired by the *prime minister*, comprising the leading *ministers* in charge of *civil service departments*, and whose *constitutional* functions are to act as a forum for discussion, to take major decisions and to resolve disagreements referred to it.

- The size of the cabinet (currently 22 members) depends on the prime minister, who also selects its membership and decides on how frequently it meets (currently once a week on Thursday mornings).

cabinet committee: a group of *cabinet* members selected by the *prime minister* to discuss and decide on a particular issue or *policy* area before reporting to the cabinet.

- Cabinet committees are used at the prime minister's discretion. The committees may be either *standing* (permanent) or ad hoc (temporary).
- Although the existence of such committees had been known about publicly for some time, *John Major* was the first prime minister to publish details concerning the structure of a system of cabinet committees and their membership.

cabinet government: the theory on the location of power in *government* that states that decision-making in the *executive* rests with the *cabinet*, chaired by the *prime minister*.

- This traditional view of the UK's *constitutional* arrangements is now out of date as a result of the increased power of the prime minister.
- *TIP* The growing infrequency of cabinet meetings is strong evidence for the absence of cabinet government, but note that the importance of the cabinet should not be understated, for example during *John Major*'s premiership.

cabinet minister: a member of the *cabinet*, appointed by the *prime minister* and usually in charge of a *department* or *ministry*.

- *e.g.* The *chancellor of the exchequer* and the *home secretary*.

Cabinet Office: central coordinating body within the *civil service* whose role is to facilitate the work of the *cabinet*.

- It is led by a *civil servant* whose position is *cabinet secretary*.
- *TIP* The Cabinet Office has been strengthened and expanded under *Tony Blair*, leading some to suggest that its more central role in the *executive* is turning it into the *prime minister*'s department.

cabinet secretary: the senior *civil servant* who heads the *Cabinet Office*.

campaign: a strategic effort mounted by a *political party* and its *candidates* to maximise their votes in an election.

- *General election* campaigns might be considered to begin as soon as the results of the previous election have been declared. Strictly, however, campaigns last 3 or 4 weeks following the announcement of the date of the general election.
- Campaigns are conducted at both a *constituency* and national level involving *canvassing*, speeches and *party election broadcasts*. Recent campaigns have adopted more sophisticated techniques using consultants, *pollsters*, *focus groups* and selective mail shots.
- There is some debate regarding the effect campaigns have on *voting behaviour* relative to other factors (see *short-term factors* and *long-term factors*).

candidate: a person seeking appointment or election.

- In elections to *parliament* the names of the candidates, selected by their *political parties* unless they are *independent* candidates, appear on the *ballot paper*.

canvassing: door-to-door visits in a *constituency* conducted by *party activists* as part of an effort to identify party support and maximise the votes cast for a party at an election.

capitalism: a society in which the economy is dominated by privately owned land and businesses.

card vote: the former practice at *Labour Party conferences* in which *delegates* from *affiliated* organisations would cast a *block vote* by holding up a card showing the number of members whose votes they were casting. See also *one member, one vote* and *block vote*.

cash for questions: the scandals that came to light in 1994 involving a number of Conservative MPs, notably Neil Hamilton, who accepted payment in exchange for asking *parliamentary questions* without declaring this in the *Register of Members' Interests* as required by the rules of *parliament*.

- The scandal formed part of a series of embarrassments for the Conservative government before the 1997 *general election*, collectively known as *sleaze*. Neil Hamilton was challenged and defeated in his *safe seat* of Tatton at the general election by the former BBC journalist Martin Bell, who ran as an *independent candidate*.
- The cash for questions scandal prompted the setting up of the *Nolan Committee*.

cause group: a type of *pressure group* (also known as a promotional group) which seeks to promote an interest or idea not of direct personal benefit to its members.

- *e.g.* The Royal Society for the Protection of Birds (RSPB) and the National Society for the Prevention of Cruelty to Children (NSPCC).
- *TIP* Be able to distinguish between cause groups and *sectional groups*.

CBI: see *Confederation of British Industry*.

Central Office: the *Conservative Party's* administrative headquarters, headed by the *party chairman*, located in *Smith Square*, London, responsible for party finances, membership and national election *campaigns*.

Centre for Policy Studies: the *right-wing think-tank* established in 1974 by *Margaret Thatcher* and Keith Joseph, sometimes described as the engine-room of *Thatcherism*.

chancellor of the exchequer: a leading member of the *cabinet* who is head of the *Treasury* and responsible for the *Budget* and economic policy in general.

e.g. Gordon Brown has been chancellor of the exchequer since 1997.

chief of staff: the political appointee who has a central coordinating role in the *Prime Minister's Office*.

chief whip: an MP, or member of the *House of Lords*, in charge of a team (the *whips' office*) who works on behalf of the party leadership to manage parliamentary business and ensure *party discipline*, particularly in terms of voting, in the parliamentary party.

- The government's chief whip in the *House of Commons* attends *cabinet* meetings.
- Hilary Armstrong has been Labour's chief whip in the House of Commons since 2001.

citizen: a person formally recognised by a *state* as a member of that state and thereby possessing certain *rights* (to vote, for example) and responsibilities (perhaps to serve in the armed forces in time of war).

- The *Maastricht Treaty* introduced the concept of *European Union* citizenship.

Citizen's Charter: *John Major*'s attempt in 1991 to provide the general public with guarantees on the provision of public services.

- A *Cabinet Office* team ran the initiative and awarded Charter Marks for the provision of high-quality public services.
- In 1998 the Labour government replaced the Citizen's Charter with the similar *Service First* initiative.

civil liberties: fundamental freedoms enjoyed by individuals or groups in society which, under normal circumstances, cannot be legally constrained by other individuals, groups or the government.

- The term is often used as a synonym for *rights*.
- The right to exercise civil liberties can be suspended in exceptional circumstances, such as during war or other national emergency.

e.g. Civil liberties include freedom of expression, freedom of religion and freedom of assembly.

civil rights: see *rights*.

civil servant: an unelected and politically neutral bureaucrat or official in the *civil service*.

- The term covers a vast range of public employees who are ultimately accountable to *parliament*.

civil service: the collective term for the government *departments, ministries* and *offices* responsible for the formulation and administration of government *policy*.

- The civil service is staffed by unelected and politically neutral *civil servants*.

▨ *TIP* The civil service is often simply referred to as *Whitehall* due to the location of its most important offices in central London.

civil society: the term describing the non-political organisation of and relationships between individuals in society.

▨ *e.g.* Civil society includes families, businesses and religions. It also includes voluntary organisations, such as environmental groups, but excludes *political parties*.

class: the social and economic division still regarded as an important factor in determining political allegiances and the way people vote. See *social class*.

class alignment: the long-term and consistent inclination of a large majority of the *electorate* to vote for the *political party* that most closely represents the interests of its *social class*. See also *class dealignment*.

● The term is used to describe the situation in which the majority of the *working class* can be relied upon to vote Labour and the majority of the *middle class* can be relied upon to vote Conservative from one election to the next.

● There is a link between class alignment and *partisan alignment*.

● Both class and partisan alignment were significant features of *voting behaviour* in the UK from 1945 until the 1970s. In the 1970s, dealignment was observed.

▨ *TIP* Note that even during periods when class alignment has been observed, there has always been a significant minority of the electorate that has voted for what others perceive as the class enemy. For example, one-third of the working-class vote has always been cast for the Conservatives.

class dealignment: the decline in the long-term and consistent inclination for a large majority of the *electorate* to vote for the *political party* that most closely represents the interests of its *social class*.

● Class dealignment has been observed in the British electorate since the 1970s. This phenomenon has coincided with a rise in the number of *floating voters* and the resulting electoral *volatility* has made predicting *voting behaviour* more difficult.

● Studies show that between 1945 and 1970 up to two-thirds of all voters voted with their natural class party. Since 1974 this has dwindled to around 45%, with increasing numbers voting for the class enemy, non-class centre parties (such as the *Liberal Democrats*) or *nationalist* parties.

class voting: the phenomenon of people voting for their natural *class* party: for example, members of the *working class* voting Labour and the *middle class* voting Conservative.

● It has been noted that class voting (*class alignment*) has been in decline since the 1970s, with increasing numbers of voters being prepared to vote for the class enemy. This is known as *class dealignment*.

Clause IV: the part of the *Labour Party*'s *constitution* — formerly containing its commitment to *nationalisation* — which was symbolically abandoned when the clause was rewritten in 1995 during the party's transformation into *New Labour*.

closed list: a feature of an *electoral system* in which voters choose between *political* *parties*, each of which publishes a list containing the same number of *candidates* standing for election in a particular area.

- This system features *proportional representation*, since each party is allocated a share of the *representatives* to be elected, beginning with the candidate at the top of the party's list, in proportion to the share of the votes cast for that party.
- *e.g.* It was introduced in the UK, with regional lists, for the 1999 *European elections*.
- *TIP* Distinguish between the closed-list system (where the voter is required to vote for a political party rather than a candidate) and the *open-list* system (which forms a part of *AV plus* and is where the voter can vote either for a political party or for a candidate from one of the lists).

CLP: see *Constituency Labour Party*.

coalition government: a government composed of members of more than one *political party*.

- Coalition governments are usually considered a practical necessity when no party has an *overall majority* in the *House of Commons* (a *hung parliament*). This situation is rare under *first-past-the-post* but far more likely under an electoral system featuring *proportional representation*, as demonstrated in other countries such as Germany. There are widely held doubts about their stability.
- *e.g.* Although coalition governments are rare in the UK, there was a coalition government during the Second World War for the purpose of promoting national unity.

co-decision procedure: shared legislative power in the *European Union* between the *European Parliament* and the *Council of Ministers*.

- The introduction of the co-decision procedure in the *Maastricht Treaty*, and its extension in the *Amsterdam Treaty*, enabled the European Parliament to reject *legislation* and thus represented a significant increase in its power.

codified constitution: an *entrenched* legal document detailing the composition and responsibilities of the institutions of government and describing their relations both with each other and with the country's *citizens*. See also *uncodified constitution*, *written constitution* and *unwritten constitution*.

- Unlike the UK, whose constitution is to be found in a variety of sources, the USA has a codified constitution, written in 1787. Whether a codified or uncodified constitution is better is the subject of debate involving questions of flexibility, reliability and certainty.

collective responsibility: a *convention* of the constitution which states that all members of the *cabinet* are collectively responsible for its decisions and which demands that they adopt a public stance of unity on government *policy* with any disagreements being kept secret.

- Failure to abide by collective responsibility can result in resignation or dismissal from the government. Collective responsibility is an aspect of *ministerial responsibility*. See also *individual responsibility*.
- *e.g.* In 1986 Michael Heseltine resigned as defence secretary because he felt that

he was not able to toe the government line on the sale of the Westland helicopter firm and that he had been prevented from putting forward his arguments in *cabinet*. During *John Major*'s time as *prime minister* there were a number of examples of the collective responsibility convention breaking down over disagreements on Europe and the *single currency*. *Euro-sceptics* such as Peter Lilley, Michael Portillo and, most notably, John Redwood, did little to hide disagreements with cabinet and were suspected of leaks in breach of cabinet secrecy, and yet retained their posts in the government. Because of Major's weak position — due to a small parliamentary *majority* and a divided party — it would have been damaging for him to dismiss such senior members of his cabinet.

■ *TIP* The nature of collective responsibility is changing. It originally applied only to the cabinet but now appears to have been extended to cover all members of the government.

Commission: see *European Commission*.

commissioner (European): a member of the *European Commission*, appointed by the government of a *member state*.

● Most member states have one commissioner; and the five largest states have two. These commissioners do not represent the governments of their member states and are expected to adopt a *supranational* attitude.

● Each European commissioner is allocated responsibility for a specific *policy* area such as the environment, agriculture or competition policy.

■ *e.g.* *Neil Kinnock* and Chris Patten are currently the UK's European commissioners.

Committee of Permanent Representatives (COREPER): the *European Union* body of senior *civil servants* from *member states* that considers proposals before they are discussed in the *Council of Ministers*.

Committee of Selection: the group of senior MPs in the *House of Commons* that chooses the members of *standing* and *select committees*.

■ *TIP* Although it is supposed to be *non-partisan*, the Committee of Selection has attracted criticism for being influenced by the *party whips*. An example of this was in July 2001 when Gwyneth Dunwoody, a Labour MP who had been critical of government *policy* in the previous *parliament*, was initially excluded from the transport select committee.

Committee of the Whole House: a sitting of the *House of Commons* or *Lords* allowing all MPs or *peers* to participate in the *committee stage* of important *bills*, including the *Budget* and bills affecting the *constitution*.

Committee on Standards in Public Life: established by *John Major* in 1994, following the *cash for questions* scandal, to investigate the issue of payments received by MPs from outside sources.

● This committee was originally chaired by Lord Nolan and, subsequently, by Lord Neill. See *Nolan Report* and *Neill Report*.

committee stage: the part of the *legislative process*, between the *second reading* and *report stage*, when a *bill* is considered in detail, usually by a *standing committee*.

- Occasionally, for bills affecting the *constitution*, such as during the passage of the *Human Rights Act*, the committee stage is held on the floor of the House rather than in a standing committee.
- The government can introduce *amendments* during the committee stage and can ensure the bill's progress through use of the *guillotine*.

common law: a body of legal precedent that is derived from decisions of judges in cases before the courts.

- Common law is a source of the UK's *constitution* distinct from *statute* law.

Commons: see *House of Commons.*

Confederation of British Industry (CBI): the umbrella group or *peak association* representing many large companies or employers, which both seeks and is sought by the government for consultation.

conference: a meeting (usually annual) of a national *political party* attended by central party officials, members of the parliamentary party and *delegates* from *constituency* parties. In the *Labour Party*, delegates from *affiliated* organisations also attend.

- The role and importance of the conference varies between political parties. Annual conferences are staged in the autumn and are designed to attract publicity. Less important conferences are held by political parties in the spring. Speeches are made by key figures in the party and there are debates on *policy*.
- *TIP* Note the *constitutional* importance of the Labour Party conference compared to the other parties, but note also its changing role, the redistribution of votes and its recent decline in significance.

consensus politics: a term describing a broad agreement between *political parties* on a range of issues resulting in continuity of *policy* following a change of government.

- *e.g.* The *postwar consensus* between the *Labour* and *Conservative Parties* was particularly evident in the 1950s.
- *TIP* Contrast with *adversarial politics*.

conservatism: a broad political *ideology* — based on beliefs in the maintenance of the traditional institutional framework of society, free enterprise, and law and order — which is usually (though not exclusively) associated with the *Conservative Party*. See also *Thatcherism, one-nation conservatism, wets* and *dries*.

Conservative Party: the party of government for most of the twentieth and much of the nineteenth century with its origins in the pre-1832 *Tory Party*. See also *conservatism*.

- The Conservative Party's success until recent *general elections* was based on not adhering to an *ideology*. Sir Ian Gilmour described its traditional philosophy as 'flexible pragmatism', although this changed with the advent of *Thatcherism*.
- The Conservative Party has traditionally appealed mainly to members of the *middle class*, although it has always also attracted a significant minority of *working-class* voters.

constituency: the geographical area represented by a *Member of Parliament*.

See also *multi-member constituency* and *single-member constituency*.

- The term can also be used to describe a section of the *electorate* represented by a *political party* or MP.

Constituency Labour Party (CLP): local party organisation, made up of *party members* resident in the *constituency*, which is linked to the national party.

- A Labour MP is responsible to the local CLP. The CLP may *deselect* its MP if it is unhappy with the way he or she is carrying out the job.

- CLPs play a part in selecting and promoting the official *Labour Party candidate* at an election. They send *delegates* to the annual *conference* who cast votes on *policy* decisions. CLPs also, jointly, control one-third of the votes in the *electoral college* for electing the Labour leader.

- **TIP** Be aware that CLPs can be a source of tension in the Labour Party as local *activists* tend to be more *left-wing* than the party leadership. This was particularly the case in the early 1980s when the influence of CLPs grew. More recently, however, tensions have been less apparent.

constituent: a resident of a *constituency* represented by a *Member of Parliament*.

constitution: a legal framework detailing the composition and responsibilities of the institutions of *government* and describing their relations both with each other and with the country's *citizens*.

- The constitutions of many countries can be found written in a single codified document (e.g. the USA). The constitution of the UK, however, comes from numerous sources, some of these unwritten customs and *conventions*.

- *Political parties* can also have constitutions. See, for example, *Clause IV* (of the *Labour Party*'s constitution).

- **TIP** Strictly speaking, the UK's is not an *unwritten constitution* but is one that is partly written but *uncodified*.

constitutional government: *government* (see abstract and general senses) which functions according to rules laid down in a *constitution* and therefore implies the operation of constraints on the exercise of power, particularly by the *executive*.

- **e.g.** Both the UK and the USA have constitutional government, although note the different types of constitution under which they operate (see *codified* and *uncodified constitution*).

constitutional reform: change to the form and content of the institutions of *government* and their legal relations both with each other and with the country's *citizens*.

- The *Labour Party*'s 1997 *manifesto* contained numerous proposals on constitutional reform that subsequently became the subject of *legislation*. The areas examined by Labour included *devolution, human rights, electoral reform* and reform of the *House of Lords*.

convention (constitutional): a generally accepted rule of constitutional practice that has evolved over time.

- **e.g.** *Individual* and *collective responsibility*.

cooperation procedure: the method of decision-making between *European Union* institutions introduced with the *Single European Act* in 1986 and replaced with the *co-decision procedure* adopted in the *Maastricht Treaty*.

● When the cooperation procedure was introduced it represented a significant increase in the *legislative* power of the *European Parliament*, enabling it to put pressure on the *Commission* and *Council of Ministers*.

core executive theory: a theory which states that *executive* decisions are taken by a network of institutions operating at the heart of *government* with the *prime minister* in a central position.

● The theory was developed by the academics P. Dunleavy and R. A.W. Rhodes in 1990 in an attempt to advance debate from the traditional focus on *prime ministerial government* versus *cabinet government*. The important elements of the core executive vary over time and according to the prime minister, but they include *cabinet committees*, the *Cabinet Office*, the *Treasury*, bilateral meetings between the prime minister and the relevant *cabinet minister*, informal ministerial meetings and interdepartmental committees.

COREPER: see *Committee of Permanent Representatives*.

corporatism: a post-Second World War style of government decision-making that involved employers and *trade unions*.

● Also known as *tripartism*, corporatism in the UK is associated with the *National Economic Development Council*, a body that was established in 1961 and abolished by *John Major* in 1993.

● As a style of governing, corporatism fell out of favour during *Margaret Thatcher*'s period in office.

councillor: an elected member of a council (either *borough, metropolitan district, county* or *district*) in *local government*.

Council of Ministers: the most important decision-making body of the *European Union*, comprising *representatives* of the governments of *member states* and carrying out *executive* and *legislative* functions.

● Originally most EU decisions were taken unanimously in the Council of Ministers, thus allowing member states a *veto* to protect their national interests. Since the *Single European Act* (1986), a system of weighted voting called *qualified majority voting* (QMV) has made the blocking of proceedings more difficult.

county council: an elected *local government* assembly, comprising *councillors* elected every 4 years with responsibilities including local planning, roads and traffic, police and fire services, refuse disposal and education.

■ *e.g.* Somerset County Council.

Cranborne Compromise: the deal negotiated in 1999 by the Labour government and the *Conservative Party*'s leader in the *House of Lords* in which 92 *hereditary peers* retained their rights to sit and vote in the chamber when *legislation* removed those rights from the majority of hereditary peers. See also *Weatherill Amendment*.

- The Conservative Party leader *William Hague* sacked Lord Cranborne for having brokered the deal behind his back.

crossbencher: an *independent* member of the *House of Lords* without party affiliation (that is not taking the *whip*), so called because of the chamber's seating arrangements.

dealignment: the breakdown of the long-term and consistent inclination to vote for a particular *political party* observed in the *electorate*. See also *alignment*.

- Both *class dealignment* and *partisan dealignment* have been observed in the electorate since the 1970s. This phenomenon has coincided with a rise in the number of *floating voters* and the resulting electoral *volatility* has made predicting *voting behaviour* more difficult.

debate: the feature of parliamentary practice in which MPs make speeches advancing opposing arguments.

- There are various types of debate. They usually concern *legislation* and take place at stages in the *legislative process*. However, a non-legislative topic for debate or motion may also be chosen on a particular issue by the government (or *opposition* parties on 20 *opposition days* in the year). A *backbench MP* may also raise an *adjournment debate*.

delegate: a person sent to a meeting or *conference* with instructions on how to vote and represent the views of those who have sent him or her.

- **e.g.** The *Labour Party conference* is made up of delegates from *Constituency Labour Parties* and *affiliated* organisations.
- **TIP** The distinction is often drawn between a delegate and a *representative*. A representative is allowed to exercise judgement on how to vote and represent the views of those who have sent him or her, whilst a delegate receives instructions.

democracy: a political system in which the people participate, usually by choosing members of the institutions of government in elections. See also *direct democracy* and *representative democracy*.

democratic deficit: the argument that government *accountability* is diminished when decisions over the administration of public policy are taken by unelected figures.

- **TIP** This argument has been advanced against some aspects of decision-making by institutions in the *European Union* and by *quangos* in the UK.

Democratic Unionist Party (DUP): the Northern Irish, Protestant and *unionist political party*, founded by Reverend Ian Paisley in 1971, which is now opposed to the *Good Friday Agreement*.

Demos: a *think-tank* established in 1993 which — although it claims to be independent and *non-partisan* — has enjoyed influence with *New Labour*.

department: a component part of the *civil service* responsible for the formulation and administration of a particular aspect of government policy, staffed by *civil servants* and headed by a *cabinet minister*.

■ **e.g.** The Department of Health and the Department of the Environment, Food and Rural Affairs.

■ **TIP** As well as departments, some parts of the civil service are known as *offices* (e.g. Northern Ireland) and others as *ministries* (e.g. Defence).

departmental select committees: the system of *House of Commons* committees established in 1979 whose function is to scrutinise the expenditure, administration and policies of individual government *departments*.

● There are currently 16 departmental select committees, each examining a government department (e.g. the Culture, Media and Sport committee chaired by the Labour MP Gerald Kaufman). Each committee has 11 members.

● Departmental select committees may call and interview witnesses from both inside and outside the government. The committees use this information in reports for presentation to the House of Commons.

● The committees were intended to operate in a *non-partisan* manner, with the membership and chairs being shared by the parties. There is evidence, however, of the influence of parties in the selection of members and the deliberations of the committees. In July 2001, for example, it was claimed that *Labour Party whips* influenced the selection of the chairman of the transport committee when the Labour MP Gwyneth Dunwoody — who had been critical of the government in the previous parliament — was removed from the post. She was later reinstated following a *backbench rebellion* by Labour MPs.

■ **TIP** Be able to distinguish between departmental and *non-departmental select committees*, some of which existed before 1979.

deposit (electoral): the sum of £500 required from each *candidate* in a parliamentary *election*.

● The idea behind electoral deposits is to deter frivolous candidates.

● The deposit is returned to those candidates who have polled at least 5% of the votes cast.

deselection: the process enabling a *constituency* party to rid itself of the sitting MP as the party's candidate at the next election.

■ **e.g.** Sir Nicholas Scott, the Conservative MP for Kensington and Chelsea, was deselected by his constituency party prior to the 1997 *general election*. This was the result of his embarrassing behaviour at the 1996 *Conservative Party conference*.

devolution: the movement of political *power* away from a central authority to other local, regional or national governments.

■ **e.g.** The creation of the *Scottish Parliament* and the *Welsh Assembly* in 1999 resulted from the *Labour Party*'s *devolution* proposals, which also included devolving power to the English regions. See also *Greater London Authority*.

d'Hondt Formula: this is used when counting votes in the *alternative member system* (and other *hybrid electoral systems* involving *party lists*) to allocate the additional *seats* that aim to ensure a degree of *proportionality*.

- The formula produces a figure for each party, with the party having the highest qualifying for an additional seat. The figure is calculated by dividing the total number of votes won by a party by the sum of one plus the number of seats already won by that party.

direct action: political activity outside the formal political process which often relies on demonstrations aimed at attracting publicity and which occasionally involves violence.

- This form of *pressure group* activity is becoming increasingly common, partly reflecting disillusionment amongst some people with the political process. This tactic is associated with some *outsider groups*.
- *e.g.* Direct action is particularly common amongst environmentalists: for instance, those protesting against the proposed Newbury bypass in 1996 and, more recently, against genetically modified crops. There have also been violent protests against globalisation, such as those at the G8 summit at Genoa, Italy, in July 2001.

direct democracy: a political system or feature of a system in which political decisions are taken by the people rather than by the *representatives* acting on their behalf.

- In a state containing a large number of people, direct democracy is rarely a practical proposition, but aspects of it can be found in the use of *referendums* (e.g. those on *devolution* in Scotland and Wales in 1997) and *initiatives* (e.g. as used in California in the USA when in 1998 the question of raising the level of tax on a packet of cigarettes by 50 cents was put to the *electorate*).
- *TIP* Be able to distinguish between direct and *representative democracy*.

dissolution: the formal conclusion of the *parliamentary session* coinciding with the *prime minister* advising the *monarch* to announce a *general election*.

district council (non-metropolitan): an elected *local government* assembly, with *councillors* elected every 4 years, having responsibilities including housing, planning, refuse collection, and leisure and recreation.

- *e.g.* South Somerset District Council.

division: a formal vote in which MPs or *peers* leave the chamber and record their votes in the *division lobbies*.

division lobby: the location adjacent to the main chamber in either the *House of Commons* or *House of Lords* where votes are cast and recorded.

dominant-party system: a political system in which many *political parties* may exist and contest *elections* but only one party tends to win and dominate government.

- *e.g.* The Liberal Democratic Party in Japan held power continuously between 1955 and 1993.

Downing Street: the official residence and office of the *prime minister* (at No. 10).

- The official residences of the *chancellor of the exchequer* and the *chief whip* are also in Downing Street (occupying numbers 11 and 12).

dries: members of the faction identified with *Margaret Thatcher*, whose *New Right* ideology dominated the *Conservative Party* from the mid-1970s.

- Margaret Thatcher labelled the opposing adherents to *one-nation conservatism* as *wets*.

Droop quota: see *quota (for STV)*.

Duncan Smith, Iain (1954–): the Conservative MP for Chingford and Woodford Green and party leader since September 2001.

- Duncan Smith was regarded as the *right-wing* and *euro-sceptic* candidate in the leadership contest when, in the final round of voting, he defeated the europhile Kenneth Clarke.

DUP: see *Democratic Unionist Party*.

early day motion (EDM): a debate tabled in the *House of Commons* to which MPs can add their names, allowing attention to be drawn to a particular issue, although there is rarely time for the motion to be debated.

EDM: see *early day motion*.

EEC: see *European Economic Community*.

election: the method for choosing *representatives* where the public expresses a preference through the casting of *votes*.

- Elections are considered essential features of a *democracy*.
- *e.g.* Members of the public in the UK are able to participate in a variety of elections, including *local elections*, *European elections*, *by-elections* and *general elections*. *Political parties* also use elections to choose their leaders.

election manifesto: see *manifesto*.

electoral college: a weighted system of voting in which certain groups are allocated a particular share of the vote.

- *e.g.* An electoral college is used for electing the leader of the *Labour Party*. It comprises the *trade unions* and other *affiliated* organisations (affiliated members), the *Constituency Labour Parties* (ordinary members), the *Parliamentary Labour Party* and *Members of the European Parliament*. Each of these three groups accounts for one-third of the votes.

electoral mandate: see *mandate*.

electoral reform: changes to the *electoral system*, particularly in the way the share of the elected *representatives* won by a *political party* reflects the share of the votes cast for that party.

- Pressure for electoral reform has been associated with the *Liberal Democrats*, who feel disadvantaged by the *first-past-the-post* system and favour a system featuring *proportional representation*.
- Since 1997, the Labour government has introduced different electoral systems for elections to the *European Parliament*, the devolved assemblies in Wales and Northern Ireland and the *Scottish Parliament*, and the *mayor* of London. It also appointed the *Jenkins Commission* to suggest reforms to the system for elections to the *Westminster Parliament*.

electoral register: the list compiled in each *constituency* containing the names of those entitled to vote in an election.

- Local authorities compile the register annually following the distribution to all households of forms that are required to be completed with the names of residents over 18 years old.

electoral system: the set of rules that governs the way *elections* operate and how the votes are counted to choose elected *representatives* and the government.

- The electoral system for the *Westminster Parliament* is called *first-past-the-post* or *simple plurality* in *single-member constituencies*.
- *TIP* Distinguish between *majoritarian,* proportional (that is, those featuring *proportional representation*) and *hybrid electoral systems*.

electorate: members of the public entitled to vote in an election.

EMU: see *European Monetary Union.*

entrenchment: the firm establishment of a law, especially a provision of the *constitution*, making its amendment more difficult than is the case with ordinary *legislation*.

- *Parliamentary sovereignty* does not allow entrenchment under the UK's constitutional arrangements.
- *TIP* It has been argued that de facto entrenchment has been established with the use of *referendums* and their effect on parliamentary sovereignty. Although constitutionally possible, it is politically unlikely that *parliament* could reverse a decision previously authorised in a referendum (such as the UK's membership of the *European Union* or *devolution* to Scotland and Wales) without holding another referendum.

Erskine May: the set of rules of parliamentary procedure, known by the name of the author of ***Parliamentary Practice***, first published in 1844.

- ***Parliamentary Practice*** is a work of authority that is regarded as a source of the British *constitution*.

EU: see *European Union.*

euro: see *single European currency.*

Euro-elections: see *European elections.*

Euroland (or euro-zone): the colloquial name for the area covering those *member states* of the *European Union* in which the *single European currency* has been adopted.

European Central Bank: the *European Union* institution responsible for setting the interest rate in those *member states* that have adopted the *single European currency*.

European Commission: the executive body of the *European Union*, comprising political appointees of the governments of the *member states*, with primary responsibility for initiating *legislation*.

- Most member states have one *commissioner;* the five largest member states have two. Commissioners do not represent the governments of their member states and are expected to adopt a *supranational* attitude. *Neil Kinnock* and Chris Patten are the UK's European commissioners.

- The Commission is scrutinised by the *European Parliament*.
- It runs the central bureaucracy of the EU. This is divided into directorates-general, each responsible for a separate *policy* area and headed by a *commissioner*, much like the government *ministries* of member states.

European Community: the name of the *European Union* before *integration* was advanced with the *Maastricht Treaty*. See also *European Economic Community*.

European Convention on Human Rights: the 1950 treaty establishing a mechanism for the judicial protection of *citizens' rights* and freedoms in those countries that became signatories.

- In 2000, the Labour government's Human Rights Act incorporated the European Convention into domestic law.
- *TIP* The convention and the associated mechanism for protection of human rights are not related to membership of the *European Union*.

European Council: the *European Union* body comprising *member states'* heads of government and the *president of the European Commission* which, ordinarily, meets twice a year.

European Court of Human Rights: the final court of appeal, based in Strasbourg, which rules on cases involving allegations of *human rights* violations brought by *citizens* of countries signatory to the *European Convention on Human Rights*.

- *TIP* The court is not an institution of the *European Union* and should be clearly distinguished from the *European Court of Justice* based in Luxembourg.

European Court of Justice: the highest court of the *European Union*, based in Luxembourg, which, in matters of EU law, is superior even to the highest courts in *member states*.

- It has 15 judges, one from each member state. It has been described as the supreme court of the EU due to its role of ensuring the uniform interpretation and application of EU law and adjudicating disputes between member states.
- *TIP* The court should be clearly distinguished from the *European Court of Human Rights*, based in Strasbourg.

European Economic Community: the name for the organisation of countries, established by the six original *member states* (Belgium, the Netherlands, Luxembourg, France, Germany and Italy) under the 1957 *Treaty of Rome*, cooperating for mutual economic benefit.

- It has now grown into the *European Union* (EU), its name since 1993.

European elections: these are held once every 5 years in *member states* of the *European Union* to choose *Members of the European Parliament* (MEPs).

- The 1999 European elections in the UK chose 87 MEPs. A total of 84 MEPs were elected in England, Scotland and Wales using a *closed list electoral system* in regions of varying size. Three MEPs were elected in Northern Ireland using the *single transferable vote* system.

European Monetary Union (EMU): the development in European *integration* advanced by the *Maastricht Treaty* (1992) and involving the creation of a *single European currency* under the control of a *European Central Bank*.

- The UK, together with two other *member states*, chose not to join EMU from the start. There is disagreement both between and within the *political parties* over whether the UK should now join. The main political parties in the UK are agreed, however, that membership must be approved in advance by a *referendum*.

European Parliament: the debating and legislative chamber of the *European Union* based in Strasbourg and Brussels and made up of *Members of the European Parliament* (MEPs) representing *constituents* in *member states*.

- The legislative powers of the European Parliament are limited, although they have expanded with the 1982 *Single European Act*, the 1992 *Maastricht Treaty* and the 1997 *Treaty of Amsterdam*. The final decision over *legislation* rests with the *Council of Ministers*.
- The European Parliament has the right to scrutinise the work of the *European Commission* and the Council of Ministers. It also has the power to dismiss the European Commission, the threat of which prompted the Commission's resignation in 1999.
- The number of MEPs elected by a member state is proportionate to its population. Germany has 99 MEPs, the UK has 87 and Luxembourg 6.
- Most MEPs sit in transnational party groupings in the chamber rather than by nationality.

European Union (EU): the name since 1993 for the organisation of countries, established by the six original *member states* as the *European Economic Community* (EEC) under the 1957 *Treaty of Rome*, cooperating largely for mutual economic benefit with shared institutions for decision-making.

- The UK became a member state of the EEC on 1 January 1973 after *Prime Minister* Edward Heath signed the Treaty of Accession in 1972.
- The EU displays both *supranationalism* and *intergovernmentalism*. In many areas, the EU takes precedence over the autonomy of its member states.
- The main institutions of the EU are the *Council of Ministers*, the *European Commission*, the *European Parliament* and the *European Court of Justice*.
- There are currently 15 EU member states (Austria, Belgium, Denmark, Finland, France, Germany, Greece, Ireland, Italy, Luxembourg, Netherlands, Portugal, Spain, Sweden and the UK) and several more hoping to join (such as Poland and Hungary).

euro-sceptic: a person holding doubts about the UK's involvement in the *European Union*, viewing further political and economic European *integration* to be at the expense of national *sovereignty*.

- Euro-scepticism is most commonly associated with, although not confined to, sections of the *Conservative Party* and, particularly, with objections to joining the *single European currency*.

euro-zone: see *Euroland*.

executive: the branch of government responsible for the day-to-day running of the *state* through the execution and administration of *policies* and laws.

▨ *e.g.* In the UK, the executive is headed by the *prime minister* and includes the *cabinet*, other government *ministers* and the *civil service*.

executive agency: an office of government that is subordinate to but sufficiently independent of its parent *Whitehall department* to allow it to carry out certain key administrative functions. See also *role responsibility*.

● The system of executive or Next Steps agencies was established following the 1988 *Ibbs Report*, named after the head of the Downing Street Efficiency Unit.

▨ *e.g.* There are well over 100 executive agencies including HM Prison Service, the United Kingdom Passport Agency and the Child Support Agency.

▨ *TIP* Executive agencies are responsible for management or operations rather than policy-making, a distinction that is not always clear.

exit poll: the collated results from questioning a *sample* of voters as they leave the *polling station* about how they have just voted at an election.

● Because exit polls usually use a larger sample than *opinion polls* and because they take place immediately after the votes are cast, rather than before, the findings of such polls are normally more reliable for predicting election results.

● Exit polls are used for detailed analysis of *voting behaviour*: for instance, examining the way different *class* and age groups vote.

expressive voting: an explanation of *voting behaviour* in which votes are cast as the result of emotional rather than rational decisions: for example, because of long-term *partisan alignment*.

▨ *TIP* Contrast with *instrumental voting*.

Fabian Society: a *think-tank* founded in 1884 by Sidney and Beatrice Webb and George Bernard Shaw with the aim of promoting gradual change to *socialism*.

- The Fabian Society played a central role in founding the *Labour Party*.
- It remains *affiliated* to the Labour Party and continues to influence its *policies*.

Factortame case: a fundamentally important legal ruling in 1991 by the *European Court of Justice* regarding the precedence of *European Union* law over *acts of parliament* and the implications for British courts.

- The case involved a Spanish-owned fishing company, Factortame Limited, which was prevented from fishing due to its failure to meet the requirements of the Merchant Fishing Act 1988. Factortame Limited argued initially in British courts, and eventually with the agreement of the European Court of Justice, that the 1988 Act was incompatible with EU law and, furthermore, that British courts had the power to suspend acts of parliament which appeared to breach EU law.

▨ *TIP* The case has important implications for the limitations on *parliamentary sovereignty*.

far left: the revolutionary ideas and *ideology* based on the philosophy of Karl Marx and associated in the UK with fringe groups such as the *Socialist Labour Party* and the *Socialist Workers' Party*.

far right: the authoritarian — often racist and nationalistic — ideas and *ideology* associated in the UK with fringe groups such as the *British National Party*.

federalism: a system of government involving a central authority with its own institutions and a number of regional authorities that exercise autonomous political *power* in defined areas of responsibility.

- The USA has a federal system with a central (or federal) government in Washington DC responsible for foreign affairs, for example, and 50 state governments with responsibility for some taxation, criminal justice etc.
- There has been much debate and some anxiety (particularly in the UK) about the impact that a federal *European Union* would have on national independence and *sovereignty*.

feelgood factor: the sense of economic well-being and general contentment amongst the *electorate*, based on optimism and perceptions of the government's competence, which influences *voting behaviour* to the benefit of the party in government.

- The feelgood factor is believed to have contributed to Conservative victories in the *general elections* of 1983 and 1987 and to have disappeared by 1997. It is also considered to have contributed towards Labour's re-election in 2001.

filibuster: a delaying tactic employed in *parliament* by an opponent of a *bill* who prevents a vote being taken by continuing to speak (often on unrelated matters) and not giving way to interruptions.

- The government can overcome this tactic in the *House of Commons* by use of the *guillotine*, a device that cuts short *debate* through the imposition of time limits.
- The term — which comes from the Spanish word for pirate — is in more common use in the US Senate, where the practice is more difficult to overcome.

first lord of the Treasury: the historic title of the *prime minister*.

first minister: the principal figure in the *executive* drawn from the devolved assemblies in Northern Ireland, Scotland and Wales.

- First ministers in the *Northern Ireland Assembly*, the *Scottish Parliament* and the *Welsh Assembly* play a similar role to the *prime minister* of the UK. They lead the executive, or government, and are chosen by virtue of leading the largest *political party* in the *legislature*.

first-past-the-post (FPTP): *electoral system* used in the UK for elections to the *Westminster Parliament* in which the winning *candidate* requires a *simple plurality* of votes (i.e. more than any other individual candidate).

- The system has been the subject of criticism and calls for *electoral reform*, particularly by those parties disadvantaged by its effects (for instance, the *Liberal Democrats*). First-past-the-post tends to deliver disproportionate results (i.e. where the share of *seats* won by a party does not reflect the share of votes won). The winning candidate in a *constituency* often polls less than half the votes cast (i.e. not an *overall majority*), which contributes to the phenomenon of *wasted votes*.

■ *TIP* First-past-the-post should strictly be described as simple plurality in *single-member constituencies*.

first reading: the start of the *legislative process* in *parliament* when a *bill* is introduced and its passage to the *second reading* is determined by a vote.

floating voter: a voter who does not show loyalty in voting for the same *political party* from one election to the next and is therefore considered as open to persuasion by the parties, particularly during election *campaigns*. See also *identifier*.

- The number of floating voters has increased with *dealignment*.
- Floating voters are particularly the focus of parties' attention in *marginal constituencies*.

focus group: a small representative *sample* (usually between eight and ten people) of the *electorate* which is consulted by a *political party* to enable it to gauge *public opinion* and discuss *policies* in some depth with potential voters.

- *New Labour*'s use of focus groups has attracted criticism from those who regard an over-reliance on such techniques as contributing to the abandonment of traditional Labour *ideology* and the adoption of policies for the sake of popularity.

Foot, Michael (1913–): the former MP and *left-wing* leader of the *Labour Party* from 1980 until his resignation following Labour's *general election* defeat in 1983.

- Although possessing unquestioned intelligence and ability as a public speaker, Foot drew criticism for the direction in which he led the Labour Party and for the left-wing *manifesto* for Labour's unsuccessful 1983 campaign. His seeming lack of awareness of the importance of public image was an anachronism in the television age.

foreign secretary: a leading member of the *cabinet* who is head of the Foreign and Commonwealth Office and is responsible for foreign *policy* and international diplomacy.

- Jack Straw was appointed foreign secretary in 2001.

franchise: the right to vote which, in the UK, includes all adults over the age of 18.

- Members of the *House of Lords*, patients detained under mental health legislation, sentenced prisoners and people convicted within the preceding 5 years of corrupt or illegal electoral practices are not eligible to vote in parliamentary *elections*.
- The franchise was gradually extended over the nineteenth and twentieth centuries.

freedom of information: the desire of campaigners for *open government*, entailing ease of access to information held by government and an end to unnecessary government secrecy.

- In line with other countries, such as the USA, the 1997 Labour *manifesto* promised a Freedom of Information Act. However, the Labour government has been accused of watering down its provisions during its passage into *legislation*.

Fresh Future: the document, published in 1998 by the Conservative leader *William Hague* and accepted in a vote of *party members*, which proposed structural changes in the *Conservative Party* and the adoption of a written *constitution*.

- Four new elements of the Conservative Party structure were created in *Fresh Future*. These were the Board, the National Convention, the National Convention Executive and the *Policy Forum*.

front bench: the team of spokesmen and women for the *government* or *opposition* in the *House of Commons* and *House of Lords*. See also *cabinet* and *shadow cabinet*.

- The term comes from the seats that *frontbenchers* occupy in the chamber where they sit.

frontbencher/frontbench MP: a *Member of Parliament*, either on the *government* or *opposition* side, who has responsibilities as a major spokesperson for the party. See also *backbencher*.

funding: see *party funding*.

fusion of powers: a feature of British government in which the three branches of government (the *executive*, the *legislature* and the *judiciary*) do not operate independently of each other.

● Because the *prime minister* (as head of the executive) is the leader of the *majority political party* in the *House of Commons* (the dominant part of the legislature), the executive can, in most circumstances, be regarded as being in control of the legislature.

▨ *TIP* The fusion of powers (the lack of a *separation of powers*) in the UK is evident from the convention that members of the *cabinet* (a part of the executive) must be members of either the House of Commons or *House of Lords* (the legislature). Indeed, the *Lord Chancellor* occupies a position in all three branches of government.

gender gap: the difference in *voting behaviour*, in terms of party support, between men and women.

- In the 1960s and 1970s it was observed that women were more likely to vote Conservative and men more likely to vote Labour. By the 1997 and 2001 *general elections*, however, these gender differences had largely disappeared. The change in voting behaviour may be explained by the *Labour Party*'s adoption of policies and strategies appealing to women voters, and an increase in the proportion of women in full-time employment who are therefore more likely to be attracted by Labour's traditional support of lower-wage earners.

general election: the day (traditionally a Thursday) chosen by the *prime minister* — after an interval of no more than 5 years since the preceding election — on which all *constituencies* elect their MPs to the *House of Commons*.

- A general election is when the *electorate* chooses a government and prime minister.
- Strictly speaking, it is the *monarch* who calls a general election on the advice of the prime minister.
- **TIP** There is a considerable advantage to the prime minister's party in being able to choose a general election date when its popularity is high. This advantage does not exist in the USA, for example, which has elections on fixed dates.

general secretary (Labour Party): the head of the national party bureaucracy, based at *Millbank Tower* in London, elected by the annual *conference* on the recommendation of the *National Executive Committee*.

gerrymandering: the practice of redrawing *constituency* boundaries, or altering a constituency social composition, in order to gain electoral advantage for a *political party*.

- The word comes from Elbridge Gerry, a nineteenth-century governor of Massachusetts, who drew a congressional district shaped like a salamander.
- Unlike in the USA — where state politicians draw congressional district boundaries — opportunities for gerrymandering in the UK are limited because the politically neutral *Boundary Commissions* draw constituency boundaries.

Westminster City Council, however, was accused of gerrymandering to the advantage of the *Conservative Party* in the 1980s when it employed a *policy* of encouraging council property residents, who were likely Labour voters, to move out of the area.

GLA: see *Greater London Authority*.

golden age of parliament: the period between the 1832 Reform Act (which removed many corrupt electoral practices and control of the *House of Commons* by the aristocracy) and the 1867 Reform Act (which extended the *franchise* and led to expanded party organisations and increased *party discipline* at *Westminster*).

- The 1832–67 golden age was characterised by the *power* and independence of individual MPs.
- Some regard this period as displaying a balance of power between the *executive* and *legislature*.

Good Friday Agreement: the 1998 multi-party negotiated settlement on the future government of Northern Ireland, which provided for a devolved *Northern Ireland Assembly* at Stormont and various forums for British–Irish and cross-border cooperation.

government (abstract sense): the system for organising a *state* that usually involves the creation, administration and adjudication of laws.

government (general sense): the body of institutions, together comprising an *executive, legislature* and *judiciary*, responsible for running the UK's internal and external affairs.

government (specific sense): the *executive* body headed by the *prime minister*, ordinarily the leader of the *majority political party* in the *House of Commons*, comprising members of the House of Commons and the *House of Lords* with responsibilities within *departments* for specific areas of *policy*.

government bill: a law proposed by the government, the passage of which through *parliament* is almost guaranteed due to the *government majority* and *party discipline* in the *House of Commons*.

- A large majority of bills proposed and passed in parliament are of this type. This is due to the government's control of the *legislative process*.

government department: see *department*.

government majority: the number of MPs from the governing party in excess of the total of all those from the other parties represented in the *House of Commons*.

- *e.g.* Following the *Labour Party*'s victory in the 2001 *general election*, the government majority was 167.

Greater London Assembly: the 25-member assembly with some responsibilities for *local* (or *regional*) *government*, which was first elected in May 2000 as part of the *Greater London Authority*.

Greater London Authority (GLA): the additional tier of *local* (or *regional*)

Home Office: the part of the *civil service* responsible for the home affairs of the UK, including the maintenance of public order, the administration of criminal justice and immigration.

home secretary: a leading member of the *cabinet* who is head of the *Home Office* and responsible for home affairs.

- The home secretary exercises certain quasi-judicial powers relating to the length of sentences to be served by prisoners and when they may be released on parole.
- *e.g.* David Blunkett has been the home secretary since 2001.

House of Commons: the elected chamber of the UK *Parliament*, the members of which are known as *Members of Parliament* (MPs).

- The House of Commons meets in the *Palace of Westminster* where it has a debating chamber, committee rooms and various offices.
- The functions of the Commons include legislating, representing the MPs' *constituents*, debating and scrutinising the government.
- Both due to its democratic credentials as the elected chamber and as a result of the *Parliament Acts (1911* and *1949)* (under which the *House of Lords* can only delay rather than veto *legislation* passed in the Commons), the House of Commons is regarded as superior to the Lords.

House of Lords: the unelected second chamber of the UK *Parliament*.

- The membership of the House of Lords is mixed. Most members now are *life peers*, together with the 92 remaining *hereditary peers*, 26 bishops of the Church of England and 12 senior judges.
- As with the *House of Commons*, the House of Lords has a debating chamber and other facilities in the *Palace of Westminster*.
- The functions of the House of Lords are similar to those of the Commons, although the representative function differs as members do not have *constituents* in the same way as MPs. There is also a judicial function performed by the judges, or *Law Lords*, who act as the country's highest court of appeal.
- Both due to its lack of democratic credentials as the unelected chamber and as a result of the *Parliament Acts (1911* and *1949)* (under which the Lords can only delay rather than veto *legislation* passed in the Commons), the House of Lords is regarded as inferior to the Commons.

human rights: see *rights*.

Human Rights Act: the law, which came into effect in 2000 as part of the Labour government's programme of *constitutional reform*, incorporated the *European Convention on Human Rights* into UK domestic law.

- The Human Rights Act is intended to provide for the better protection of *citizens' rights* and freedoms through domestic courts rather than involving a lengthy process of appeal to the *European Court of Human Rights* in Strasbourg.

hung parliament: the situation, usually as the result of a *general election*, in which no one *political party* has an *overall majority* of MPs in the *House of Commons*.

- A hung parliament means there cannot be a *majority government* and the outcome will, therefore, usually be the formation of a *minority* or *coalition government.* A hung parliament often implies instability because of the lack of a clear winning party and the time taken to form a government following a general election.

- Hung parliaments are rare under the current UK *electoral system.* The February 1974 general election is the only one to have produced a hung parliament since the Second World War. Under a more *proportional electoral system,* hung parliaments would be more likely because of the rarity of a party achieving 50% of the votes (and therefore 50% of the seats in the Commons). Both the *Scottish Parliament* and the *Welsh Assembly* were hung after the elections in 1999.
- The term can also describe *local councils* in which no one party has an overall majority.

hustings: both campaigning and election proceedings in general.

- This is a figurative term taken from the wooden platform from which *candidates* used to address *electors* in parliamentary elections.

hybrid electoral system: a mixed voting system including features from two or more separately identifiable *electoral systems.*

- A hybrid system allows for the inclusion of desirable features from different electoral systems.
- *e.g.* Examples are the *additional member system* (which includes both *proportional representation* through *party lists* and representation through *single-member constituencies*) and *AV plus.*

Ibbs Report: the report recommending structural changes to the *civil service*, officially known as *Improving Management in Government: The Next Steps*, published in 1988 by Sir Robert Ibbs, the head of the Downing Street Efficiency Unit.

- The report's main recommendation was the creation of a system of *executive agencies* (or Next Steps agencies) to carry out operational or administrative functions.

identification (party): the long-term attachment to a *political party* resulting in loyal support in voting for that party. See also *alignment*.

identifier: a *voter* with a consistent attachment or loyalty to a *political party*.

■ *TIP* Increased *volatility* in the *electorate* combined with the decline in *partisanship* (i.e. the fall in number of party identifiers) has magnified the importance of *short-term factors* since the 1970s.

ideological voting model: a theory on *voting behaviour* that a voter's personal *ideology* and that a voter's perception of a *political party*'s values and ideology help determine the way he or she votes.

- The model was developed by academics A. Heath et al. in *How Britain Votes* (1985). It continues to have its adherents but has drawn criticism for its failure to explain why the *Labour Party* did not attract more votes in the 1980s despite *opinion poll* evidence showing that a majority of voters were prepared to pay higher taxes to improve public services (i.e. holding common ideological positions).

■ *TIP* The ideological voting model is a variant of the *issue voting model*. It argues that a voter's ideology is a more important determinant of party attachment and voting behaviour than a voter's attitude towards certain key issues.

ideologue: someone guided by a clear and consistent political philosophy or *ideology*.

- Few voters and *politicians* can be described as ideologues.

■ *e.g.* John Redwood and Sir Keith Joseph before him have been described as *New Right* ideologues.

ideology: a guiding set of core political, economic and social beliefs or values.

- Individuals, *political parties* and other organisations can adhere to ideologies. An ideology can influence the way a voter votes (see *ideological voting model*) and the *policies* a political party adopts.

■ *e.g.* *Socialism* has been an influential ideology in the *Labour Party*. *Neo-liberalism* became an influential ideology in the *Conservative Party* from the 1970s onwards.

incumbency: the status and resulting advantages of an *incumbent* when seeking re-election.

● In US Congressional elections, where the advantages of incumbency are more apparent than in UK parliamentary elections, challengers rarely succeed in unseating incumbents.

■ *TIP* Until recently, incumbency has not been considered an important factor in UK elections. However, it was influential in the 2001 *general election*, when only 21 *constituencies* changed the *political party* of their MP. The major parties increased their share of the vote most when defending their most *marginal seats*. For example, in Torbay the *Liberal Democrats* increased their *majority* from 12 to 6,708.

incumbent: current office-holder such as a sitting MP. See *incumbency*.

Independence Party (UK): see *UK Independence Party*.

independent: a *candidate* or elected MP who is not a member of, and does not represent, a *political party*.

● Successful independent candidates are rare in the UK because they fight without the advantages of major party support and organisation. A vote for an independent is often regarded as wasted because it does not directly contribute to the election of a government.

■ *e.g.* Martin Bell, elected as the MP for Tatton in 1997, is a rare example of a successful independent candidate. He ran as an anti-sleaze candidate against the Conservative Neil Hamilton (see *cash for questions*), without the Labour and Liberal Democrat parties fielding candidates. Bell lost in the 2001 *general election* when he stood in the Brentwood and Ongar *constituency*. Richard Taylor, elected as the MP for Wyre Forest in 2001, is another example of a successful independent candidate. He campaigned against National Health Service cuts and defeated the sitting Labour MP.

■ *TIP* Independents in the *House of Lords* are known as *crossbenchers*.

individual responsibility: a *convention* of the *constitution* which states that *ministers* are answerable to *parliament* for their conduct, for the performance of their *department* and for the actions and omissions of subordinates in the department. See also *collective responsibility*.

● Individual responsibility is an aspect of *ministerial responsibility*. Failure to abide by individual responsibility can result in resignation or dismissal from the government.

● The academic R. Pyper divides individual responsibility into 'personal responsibility' (Ron Davies resigned as Welsh secretary in 1998 following what he called a 'moment of madness' on Clapham Common) and 'role responsibility' (Lord Carrington resigned as foreign secretary in 1982 following the Argentine invasion of the Falkland Islands). This distinguishes between a *minister*'s private life and professional duties.

■ *TIP* In 1995, *home secretary* Michael Howard sacked Derek Lewis from his job as director of the Prison Service agency. Howard thus held a subordinate responsible for failings in government, which some commentators considered were attributable to him personally. This revealed that the convention of individual responsibility had become problematical with the creation of *executive agencies*.

initiative: a question put to voters, the answer to which places an obligation on the government to act, often through *legislation*.

● An initiative differs from a *referendum* in that the *electorate* demands the right to be asked the question on an issue, usually through a constitutionally recognised *petition*.

● Initiatives can be features of a *direct democracy*.

■ *TIP* There is no place for initiatives in the constitutional arrangements of the UK. Initiatives are used in Switzerland and some states in the USA.

inner cabinet: an informal group of senior *cabinet ministers* consulted by the *prime minister* in preference to the full *cabinet*.

● An advantage of relying on such a small informal grouping is that it leads to more efficient decision-making.

● The existence of such informal groups has been noted for some time under different *prime ministers*. Derek Draper, a journalist and former special *adviser*, claims that *Tony Blair* considered the creation of a formal inner cabinet.

■ *TIP* The use of an inner cabinet by a prime minister can, at the very least, give the impression of a lack of wide consultation and has implications for the operation of *cabinet government*.

insider group: a type of *pressure group* which is particularly influential because it is regularly consulted by the *ministers* and *civil servants* who make *policy* in the area in which it has an interest.

● Academic Wyn Grant distinguishes between insider and *outsider groups* on the basis of whether or not they enjoy access to government decision-makers.

● Grant distinguishes between the 'high-profile insider', the 'low-profile insider' and the 'prisoner group', the last of which is defined by becoming so closely associated with a government policy that its own reputation is harmed if the policy fails.

● Grant also sub-divides insider groups into 'institutions within the state apparatus' (e.g. the Church of England) and 'external groups' (e.g. *trade unions*, whose regular close contact with government has declined since the 1970s). Academics W. Maloney et al. also identify 'core insiders' (e.g. the NFU), 'specialist insiders' (e.g. the British Poultry Federation) and 'peripheral insiders' (e.g. Greenpeace).

■ *e.g.* The National Farmers' Union (NFU) is in regular contact with the Department for the Environment, Food and Rural Affairs because the government needs its expertise and cooperation. The NFU is therefore regarded as enjoying insider status. Concern that the interests of consumers were suffering due to this influence of food producers was part of the reason behind the establishment of the Foods Standards Agency.

■ *TIP* Be able to distinguish between insider and outsider groups.

Institute for Public Policy Research: a *think-tank*, established in 1988, which is opposed to *neo-liberal* thinking and which has influenced the *Labour Party* on social and education *policies*.

Institute of Economic Affairs: a *think-tank*, established in 1955, which believes in free-market economics and which gained influence in the *Conservative Party* during *Margaret Thatcher's* leadership.

instrumental voting: an explanation of *voting behaviour* in which votes are cast as the result of rational decisions after consideration of a party's *ideology* and *policies* and the qualities of its leader.

● Instrumental voting is central to the *rational choice model*.

■ *TIP* Contrast instrumental voting with *expressive voting*.

integration (European): the gradual unification of *European Union member states* through closer cooperation on economic and other *policies* and the strengthening of the EU's political institutions.

● Integration has been advanced by treaties signed at *Maastricht* and *Amsterdam*.

● *Euro-sceptics* object to further European integration.

interest group: see *pressure group* and *sectional group*.

intergovernmentalism: cooperation between governments of *European Union member states* without abandoning their national interests, which finds expression mainly in the EU *Council of Ministers*.

IRA: see *Irish Republican Army*.

Irish Republican Army (IRA): the armed force that waged a military campaign aimed at removing British soldiers from Northern Ireland and unifying the island of Ireland under a government in Dublin.

● The IRA has close links to *Sinn Fein*.

issue network: see *policy network*.

issue of writs: the formal *House of Commons* announcement that a *by-election* or a *general election* is to take place.

issue voting model: a theory on *voting behaviour* which holds that voting is the result of a rational assessment of the key issues of the day, the *political parties'* attitudes towards them and the *policies* directed at them.

● The model recognises the decline in *class* and *partisan alignment* observed in the *electorate* since the 1970s, and its supporters rely on it to explain the Conservative *general election* victories between 1979 and 1992.

● The issue voting model forms part of the *rational choice model*.

■ *TIP* The model's detractors point out its inadequacies in explaining why support for a party's position on an important issue does not necessarily result in a vote for that party. This was demonstrated in the 1983, 1987 and 1992 elections when Labour's policies attracted public support but failed to deliver votes.

Jenkins Commission: the five-member *commission* chaired by Lord Jenkins of Hillhead and established by the Labour government in 1997 to recommend changes to the *electoral system* for elections to the *House of Commons*.

- The commission's brief was to observe the requirement of broad *proportionality*, the need for stable government, an extension of voter choice and the retention of a link between MPs and their *constituencies*. The *Jenkins Report* (1998) recommended the adoption of *AV plus*.
- Lord (Roy) Jenkins is a former Labour *cabinet minister*, a founder member of the *Social Democratic Party* and a former leader of the *Liberal Democrats* in the *House of Lords*. He has been a long-time campaigner for *electoral reform*.

Jenkins Report (1998): this recommended the adoption of a new *electoral system*, *AV plus*.

- Under AV plus, MPs would be elected in one of two ways. The majority would be elected in *single-member constituencies* using the *alternative vote*. To ensure greater *proportionality* than at present, a minority of between 15 and 20% of top-up MPs would be elected from regional *open party lists* of *candidates*. The voter would cast two votes on the *ballot paper*, one constituency and one list vote.
- The Labour government promised to seek the *electorate*'s view on the adoption of AV plus in a *referendum*.

Joint Cabinet Committee on Constitutional Reform: an innovation in *Tony Blair*'s system of *cabinet committees* after 1997 in which the *Liberal Democrats* were represented alongside members of the Labour government.

- This was regarded as a significant development because membership of cabinet committees is traditionally confined to government *ministers*.
- The Liberal Democrats have long been interested in *constitutional reform* and their involvement in this committee was regarded as indicative of the emphasis Labour placed on this aspect of its programme.
- ▧ *TIP* The committee is an example of the closer cooperation between Labour and the Liberal Democrats fostered by Tony Blair and *Paddy Ashdown*. Note, however, that the involvement of Liberal Democrats in the committee came to an end in September 2001 due to growing disillusionment with the pace and direction of reform.

judicial independence: the freedom of judges (the *judiciary*) to make decisions without the influence of the *executive* or *legislative* branches of government. See also *judicial neutrality* and *judicial review*.

● An independent judiciary is considered essential for the maintenance of *democracy* and is a feature of the *separation of powers*.

● *TIP* Any influence able to be exercised by the other branches of government over the appointment and dismissal of judges is important when considering judicial independence.

judicial neutrality: the absence of bias amongst judges, either in favour of or against a *political party*, providing for independent decision-making by the *judiciary*.

● To retain public confidence, it is important that the judiciary operates in a *non-partisan* manner, particularly when exercising *judicial review*.

judicial review: the power exercised by law courts to supervise officials of the government and other public bodies which enables the courts to declare illegal any actions which they consider unauthorised by law (or *ultra vires*).

● The judicial review process is not automatic. An aggrieved individual or organisation must apply to the High Court for a judicial review.

● The incorporation of the *European Convention on Human Rights* in the 2000 *Human Rights Act* has extended judicial review in the UK courts to enable judges to make a 'declaration of incompatibility' when a UK law is in breach of the convention.

● *e.g.* Michael Howard, the Conservative *home secretary* in the 1990s, was found to have acted unlawfully on several occasions, including when he delayed referring the cases of *IRA* prisoners to a parole board.

● *TIP* The scope of judicial review is limited in the UK by the doctrine of *parliamentary sovereignty*. This is not the case in the USA where judicial review by the Supreme Court can declare an Act of Congress (the equivalent of an *act of parliament*) unconstitutional, thereby invalidating it.

judiciary: the branch of government responsible for the interpretation and enforcement of laws through the courts.

● In the UK, the judiciary is organised into a hierarchy of courts from magistrates courts, to county courts, to crown courts, to the High Court and the Court of Appeal. The *House of Lords*, acting in its judicial capacity, is the highest court in the UK.

junior minister: a government member below the rank of *cabinet minister*, with specific responsibilities within a *department*.

● There are three ranks of junior minister: *ministers of state, parliamentary under-secretaries* and *parliamentary secretaries*.

● The number and responsibilities of junior ministers have increased since the 1960s.

● *e.g.* In the *Home Office* there is a junior minister who is responsible for prisons. In the Department for Culture, Media and Sport there is a junior minister whose title is minister for sport.

Kennedy, Charles (1959–): the Liberal Democrat MP for Ross, Skye and Inverness West and leader of the *Liberal Democrats* since 1999.

- Kennedy was originally elected MP for Ross, Cromarty and Skye in 1983 as a member of the *Social Democratic Party*.
- He is regarded as being less favourably inclined towards cooperation with the Labour government than was his predecessor, *Paddy Ashdown*.

Kinnock, Neil (1942–): the former Labour MP for Bedwellty, leader of the *Labour Party* from 1983 to 1992 and a European *commissioner* since 1994.

- Originally on the *left wing* of the Labour Party and a protégé of *Michael Foot*, Neil Kinnock moved to the centre and, as leader, was responsible for starting the process of internal reforms continued by his successors *John Smith* and *Tony Blair*.
- Kinnock resigned as Labour Party leader following the party's *general election* defeat of 1992. This was his second defeat as Labour leader.

kitchen cabinet: a loose and informal group of advisers and friends, not necessarily in official positions, which a *prime minister* may consult.

- *e.g.* *Margaret Thatcher* is said to have relied on advice from a kitchen cabinet which included Professor Sir Alan Walters (who advised on economic matters) and Sir Robert McAlpine (a prominent businessman).
- *TIP* The term can be used disparagingly by *ministers* who resent the access and influence of such policy advisers.

Labour Party: *political party* with its origins in the nineteenth century which was created by the *trade union* movement and *socialist* organisations, such as the *Fabian Society*, to provide parliamentary representation for the *working class*.

- The Labour Party's first *prime minister*, in a *minority government*, was Ramsay MacDonald in 1924. The party won its first *overall majority* under Clement Attlee in 1945.
- Its socialist *ideology* evolved throughout the twentieth century, particularly during its transformation into *New Labour* in the 1990s.
- In the 2001 *general election,* Labour won a second consecutive full term in government for the first time in its history.

Labour Reform Group: a committee, established in 1996 and comprising over 100 Labour *backbench MPs*, which seeks to communicate the views of its members to the party leadership.

Law Lords: senior judges who are *life peers* of the *House of Lords* (and more correctly known as Lords of Appeal in Ordinary) and whose work is to carry out the chamber's judicial function in acting as the highest court of appeal in the UK.

leader of the House: the *cabinet* members from the *House of Commons* and the *House of Lords* who are responsible for organising parliamentary business, in particular the passage of government *legislation*.

- *e.g.* Robin Cook has been leader of the Commons and Lord Williams of Mostyn the leader of the Lords since 2001.

leader of the opposition: the leader of the *political party* with the second largest number of MPs, after the governing party, in the *House of Commons*.

- The opposition leader's most visible role is at *Prime Minister's Question Time*, when he or she has priority in asking questions seeking to scrutinise the *prime minister* and expose government failings.
- The leader of the opposition receives a salary in addition to that earned as an MP.

left: see *left-wing*.

left-wing: the radical ideas and *ideology* associated with *socialism*, stressing the collective interest of the community above that of the individual, and the redistribution of wealth to benefit the disadvantaged *working class*.

TIP Political ideology is often portrayed as a spectrum of opinion with *political parties* arranged along it from left to right. Because political parties themselves also contain ranges of opinion, each one has its left-wing and *right-wing* elements.

legislation: laws ordinarily created by *parliament* by the process of debating and scrutinising a *bill*, and voting on its passage into an *act of parliament* or *statute*.

● Legislation can also be created by an *Order in Council*, though this is rare.

legislative process: the way in which *legislation* is created during its passage through *parliament* and the transformation from a *bill* into an *act of parliament*.

● The legislative process in parliament follows a strict route through each house (with important bills starting in the *House of Commons*) of *first reading, second reading, committee stage, report stage* and *third reading* before a bill receives *royal assent*.

TIP The UK's legislative process — unlike in the USA — is dominated by the *executive* (or government) due to its *majority* in the House of Commons, strict *party discipline* and the subordinate role of the *House of Lords*.

legislature: the branch of government responsible for the creation of *legislation*, the product of the *legislative process*.

● Legislatures, such as the UK's *Westminster Parliament*, may also perform a representative function (where elected members look after the interests of their *constituents* and a *scrutiny* function, overseeing the actions of the *executive*.

● The UK has a *bicameral* (two chambers) legislature comprising the *House of Commons* and the *House of Lords*.

legitimacy: the legal right to govern or hold a position of *authority*.

e.g. The Labour government claims legitimacy because it was elected at the 2001 *general election*.

levy: see *political levy*.

levy plus: the *Labour Party* scheme to allow individual members of an organisation (usually a *trade union*) *affiliated* to a *Constituency Labour Party* to cast a vote in the selection of a parliamentary *candidate*.

● This voting right is conferred on those who pay a sum in addition to the *political levy* paid by the organisation of which he or she is a member.

● The scheme was introduced in 1993 at the same time as *one member, one vote* to enable individual members of affiliated organisations to participate in the selection of parliamentary candidates.

Liaison Committee: the *select committee* of the *House of Commons* which oversees the work of the select committee system and which is made up of all the committees' chairpersons.

● An example of the committee's work is **Shifting the Balance**, a report published in 2000 to consider the relationship between the *executive* and *select committees*.

Liberal Democrats: this party was created in 1988 by the merger of the *Liberal Party* and the *Social Democratic Party*.

- The Liberal Democrat Party is the *third party* in British politics, behind the *Conservative* and *Labour Parties*.
- The two founding parties of the Liberal Democrats fought the 1983 and 1987 *general elections* together as the Alliance. On merger they were first known as the Social and Liberal Democrats (SLD).
- Partly due to its roots being in two parties, the *ideology* of the Liberal Democrats is difficult to characterise, although *liberalism* and *social democracy* certainly feature. The party is often simplistically considered to occupy the middle ground of British politics, being neither on the *left wing* nor the *right*.

liberalism: a political *ideology* based on beliefs in personal liberty, tolerance and limited government which is usually, though not exclusively, associated with the old *Liberal Party*.

Liberal Party: the *third party* in British politics for most of the twentieth century until its merger with the *Social Democratic Party* in 1988 to form the *Liberal Democrats*.

- The Liberal Party emerged in the nineteenth century with its roots in the Whig Party and the Peelites (who broke away from the *Conservative Party*). Its last *prime minister* of a *majority government* was Herbert Asquith from 1908 until the party split under David Lloyd George in 1916.

life peer: a member of the *House of Lords* whose title and rights to sit and vote in the chamber are not hereditary but cease upon death.

- The *monarch* appoints life peers on the advice of the *prime minister*. Their appointment is an important aspect of prime ministers' power of *patronage*, through which they can seek to influence the composition of the House of Lords to their party's advantage.
- Since the removal of all but 92 *hereditary peers* in 1999, most members of the House of Lords have been of this type. There are currently 559 life peers in the House of Lords.

Life Peerages Act (1958): *legislation* allowing *House of Lords* membership for a new type of *peer* (*life peer*) whose title and rights to sit and vote in the chamber are not hereditary but cease upon death.

- Under the provisions of this act, women, for the first time, could become members of the House of Lords.
- Since the passage of the act, very few new *hereditary peers* have been created. In 1999 all but 92 of the hereditary peers lost the rights to sit and vote in the *House of Lords*.

lobby: this term, which refers to the areas in the *Palace of Westminster* where MPs congregate outside the debating chamber, has two meanings: as a noun, defining the privileged group of journalists who are described under *lobby system*; as a verb, describing the activity of those who seek to influence government decision-making, described under *lobbying firm*.

lobby correspondent: a political journalist working in the *lobby system*.

lobby group: an alternative term for *pressure group*.

lobbying firm: an organisation which, for a fee, arranges contacts between interested parties (often *pressure groups*) and those in a position to influence decision-making in government (*ministers, civil servants* and MPs).

- Employees of lobbying firms often have contacts and experience gained from previous employment in, or close to, government circles.
- MPs' relationships with lobbying firms are now closely regulated by the *Parliamentary Commissioner for Standards*, following the 1995 *Nolan Report*.
- *e.g.* In the *cash for questions* scandal, contact between Mohamed Al Fayed and Neil Hamilton MP was arranged by the (now defunct) lobbying firm Ian Greer Associates.

lobby system: the arrangement involving approximately 150 political journalists (or *lobby correspondents*) who are given privileged information (often more frequently than once a day) by a government representative.

- Supporters of the lobby system claim that it provides the public with information they might otherwise not receive.
- The lobby system has attracted criticism for the way in which it allows the government to control information presented to the media in unattributable, off-the-record briefings (allowing only the use of phrases such as 'a government source' or 'a Labour source'). Critics also point to the reliance of journalists on these briefings and the lack of independent investigation.
- After 1997, the *prime minister's press secretary*, Alastair Campbell, was prepared to give more briefings on the record, allowing *lobby correspondents* to attribute information to 'the prime minister's official spokesman'.

local council: an elected *local government* assembly that can be either *borough, district, metropolitan district* or *county*.

local democracy: participation by the people in government at a local level usually through *local elections*.

- The extent to which *local government* provides for local democracy depends on the powers of the institutions of local government and the levels of public participation in elections and decision-making at a local level.
- *TIP* It is felt by some that local democracy could be extended by the use of *referendums*.

local election: a *local council* election which can take place either at the same time as a *general election* or between general elections.

- *Turnout* at local elections is lower than for general elections and different, local, factors can influence *voting behaviour*. *Protest votes* against the party in government at *Westminster* are common when the local election takes place between general elections.

local government: the generic term to describe the machinery involving *local councils* and local authorities which administer a budget and provide local services such as police and fire, refuse collection and education.

long-term factors: the enduring influences affecting *voting behaviour* which, because they are not usually subject to change from one election to the next, contribute to stability in the *electorate* and predictability of results. See also *short-term factors*.

- Long-term factors such as class, religion, gender and the region in which the voter lived were considered to dominate amongst the various influences affecting voting behaviour until the 1970s.

Lord Chancellor: the senior judge and member of the government who, as head of the *judiciary*, has significant influence over the appointment of judges.

■ *TIP* The Lord Chancellor's role demonstrates the lack of a *separation of powers* in the British political system. As a senior judge, the Lord Chancellor can take part in judicial proceedings (judiciary), is the presiding officer in the *House of Lords* (part of the *legislature*), and is a member of the *cabinet* (part of the *executive*).

Lord Chief Justice: the senior judge who heads both a division of the High Court (the Queen's Bench) and the Criminal Division of the Court of Appeal.

Lords: see *House of Lords*.

lords of appeal in ordinary: see *Law Lords*.

lords spiritual: the archbishops of Canterbury and York and the 24 most senior bishops of the Church of England, who are members of the *House of Lords* as long as they hold their posts within the Church.

lords temporal: all members of the *House of Lords* who are not *lords spiritual*.

loyalist: the term used in Northern Irish politics to describe support for and a supporter of the province remaining a part of the UK.

Maastricht, Treaty of (1992): formally known as the Treaty on European Union and signed by *member states* on 7 February 1992, it set out the structural changes to advance *integration* and transform the *European Community* into the *European Union*.

- The most important elements of the Maastricht Treaty were to establish a programme for *European Monetary Union* (EMU) (including the adoption of a *single European currency*) to strengthen the role of the *European Parliament*, and to extend the use of *qualified majority voting* (QMV) in the *Council of Ministers*, thereby removing a member state's veto over additional *policy* areas.
- *John Major*'s government faced determined opposition from *euro-sceptic* Conservative *backbenchers* during the passage through the *House of Commons* of the *bill* incorporating the Maastricht Treaty.

Major, John (1943–): former Conservative MP for Huntingdon, leader of the *Conservative Party* and *prime minister* from 1990 to 1997.

- Major enjoyed rapid promotion under *Margaret Thatcher* and many regarded his succession as both party leader and prime minister as signalling a continuation of *Thatcherism*. His style of leadership, however, was more consultative.
- After the 1992 *general election* — which the Conservatives won with a narrow *majority* — Major struggled to contain disagreements within both his *cabinet* and his party over *policy* towards the *European Union*. His popularity fell after Black Wednesday, when the UK was forced to drop out of the Exchange Rate Mechanism, and it failed to recover. Major suffered a heavy defeat in the 1997 general election and resigned the leadership of the party.

majoritarian (or majority) electoral system: an *electoral system* in which a winning *candidate* must attract more than half of the votes cast in a *constituency*.

- *e.g.* Majoritarian systems such as the *alternative vote* and *supplementary vote systems* operate in *single-member constituencies*. They do not feature *proportional representation*. *First-past-the-post* is not considered a majoritarian system, since the winning candidate needs only to win more votes than the next best candidate and not necessarily more than half the votes cast.
- *TIP* Be able to distinguish between majoritarian, *hybrid* and *proportional electoral systems*.

majority: the winning margin in terms of the number of votes won by an individual *candidate* in a single *constituency*, or the number of seats in the *House of Commons* held by different *political parties* after a *general election*. See also *overall majority* and *simple majority*.

- Note that in a single constituency the majority is expressed as the difference, in terms of votes polled, between the winning candidate and the next best candidate (and not all the other *candidates* added together). Thus, in the Winchester *by-election* in November 1997 Mark Oaten's majority was 21,550 (the difference between his 37,000 votes and Gerry Malone's 15,450 votes, ignoring the 1,928 votes cast for other candidates).
- After the 2001 general election, the Labour government held a majority of 167 *seats* in the House of Commons, meaning that the party had 167 more MPs than all the other parties added together.
- When votes in *parliament* are recorded, the margin of victory (ordinarily for the government) is reported in terms of an *overall majority* of a number of votes.

majority government: a government composed of members of one *political party* as a result of that party winning more *seats* in the *House of Commons* at a *general election* than all the other parties added together. See also *coalition government* and *minority government*.

- This is the norm for governments in the UK, largely due to the effects of the *electoral system*.
- *e.g. Tony Blair*'s governments since 1997 have been majority governments.

mandate: the idea that the winning *political party* at a *general election* receives the permission of the *electorate* to govern in accordance with its promises, particularly through the passage of the legislative programme detailed in its *manifesto*.

- A mandate can be regarded as a contractual relationship between the winning party and the electorate because it contains an element of obligation on the part of the governing party which people voted for on the understanding that it would carry out its electoral promises.
- *e.g.* Following its victory in the 2001 general election, the *Labour Party* can claim a mandate to increase the minimum wage to £4.20 per hour because this was promised in the party's manifesto and — at least in theory — the voters approved this *policy*.

mandatory reselection: see *reselection*.

manifesto: a pre-election document containing a *political party*'s *policy* pledges and proposals for *government legislation*.

- A party's manifesto is the subject of attention during a *general election campaign* as it contains the promised legislative programme were the party to win the election and form the government.
- The drafting of the manifesto is often contentious, with the party leadership reluctant to take instructions as to its contents.

marginal (or marginal constituency): a parliamentary *constituency* that is usually won with a small *majority* and is therefore regarded by *political parties* as an important focus for their election *campaigns*. See also *target seat* and *safe seat*.

- Because marginal constituencies are more likely to change hands at a *general election* than seats where the result is more predictable, they receive more attention from the competing political parties and the *media*. In marginals, the parties target *floating voters*.

- **e.g.** The constituency of Rugby and Kenilworth is regarded as a Labour/Conservative marginal because both parties have a realistic chance of winning the seat in an election. Three-way marginals, where three parties have a realistic chance of winning, are rare. The results of the 2001 *general election* suggest that Bristol West is a Labour/Liberal Democrat/Conservative marginal.

mayor: traditionally the head of a *borough council* or city (in some large cities known as lord mayor).

- In May 2000, London voters elected Ken Livingstone as the city's first elected mayor. The mayor and the *Greater London Assembly* were elected at the same time, and make up the *Greater London Authority* (GLA). The GLA has a budget of over £3 billion and has some responsibility for planning and transport.

- The Labour government's stated intention is to introduce elected mayors in other cities (e.g. Birmingham, Liverpool and Middlesbrough) subject to local approval in *referendums*.

McKenzie thesis: Robert McKenzie's analysis of British *political parties*, written in 1955, in which he argued that — whatever the appearance — the *Conservative* and *Labour Parties* were dominated by their leaders with *party members* and organisations merely playing supportive roles.

- **TIP** The concentration of power in the leadership of the Conservative Party has long been recognised, but the position in the Labour Party is more open to debate. Since 1955, the dominance of the Labour leadership has increased, particularly with the internal reforms from the mid-1980s onwards, but it remains the case that the support of *conference* is required for major decisions.

media: television, radio, newspapers, the internet and other forms of mass communication.

- The broadcast media in the UK (i.e. television and radio) are under a legal obligation not to show party political bias (see *party election broadcasts*).

- The influence of the newspapers in British politics is the subject of much academic study, particularly regarding *voting behaviour*. Ownership of newspapers and support for *political parties* is given as evidence of media bias. Traditionally, this bias favoured the *Conservative Party*. However, during the 2001 *general election*, the **Daily Telegraph** was the only national daily newspaper to offer a clear endorsement of the Conservatives. *Tony Blair* and the *Labour Party* have successfully developed relations with Rupert Murdoch, the owner of the **Sun**, **The Times**, **The Sunday Times** and the **News of the World**.

- **TIP** Note that the media include more than just television, although television is seen as the most important in terms of imparting political information.

Member of Parliament (MP): a *representative* of a parliamentary *constituency* elected to the *House of Commons* for a term not exceeding 5 years, before re-election, using the *electoral system* known as *first-past-the-post* (or *simple plurality* in *single-member constituencies*).

- An MP represents both *constituents* and a *political party* (it is rare for an MP to be elected as an *independent* and not to be a *party member*). An MP is expected to assist constituents with problems related to government (see *redress of grievances*) and to vote with his or her party in the House of Commons (see *party discipline* and *whip*).
- There are currently 659 MPs representing *constituencies* in the UK.

Member of the European Parliament (MEP): a *representative* elected to the *European Parliament* in Strasbourg by voters in *European Union member states* for a term of 5 years (before re-election).

- As is the case for an MP, an MEP represents both *constituents* and a *political party*. An MEP is expected to assist constituents with problems related to the responsibilities of EU government and to vote with his or her party in the European Parliament. Most MEPs sit in transnational party groupings in the chamber rather than by nationality.
- There are currently 626 MEPs, representing voters in the 15 member states of the EU.
- The UK sends 87 MEPs to the European Parliament. In the 1999 *European elections*, a *closed-list electoral system* was used with England, Scotland and Wales, divided into 12 *multi-member constituencies*, each electing a number of MEPs according to size of population. Northern Ireland elected three MEPs using the *single transferable vote*.

Member of the Scottish Parliament (MSP): a *representative* elected to the *Scottish Parliament* in Edinburgh for a term of 5 years (before re-election).

- As is the case for an MP, an MSP represents both *constituents* and a *political party*. An MSP is expected to assist constituents with problems related to the responsibilities of the Scottish Parliament and to vote with his or her party in the Scottish Parliament.
- MSPs elect, from amongst their number, a *first minister* for Scotland.
- There are 129 MSPs elected using a *hybrid electoral system*, with 73 elected in *single-member constituencies* and 56 elected in eight multi-member *constituencies* from *party lists* to ensure a greater degree of *proportionality*. The voter may cast two votes, one for a candidate in a single-member constituency and one for a party list in a multi-member constituency.

Member of the Welsh Assembly: a *representative* elected to the *Welsh Assembly* in Cardiff for a term of 5 years (before re-election).

- As is the case for an MP, a Member of the Welsh Assembly represents both *constituents* and a *political party*. A Member of the Welsh Assembly is expected to assist constituents with problems related to the responsibilities of the Welsh Assembly and to vote with his or her party in the Welsh Assembly.

- *Members of the Welsh Assembly* elect, from amongst their number, a *first minister* for Wales.
- There are 60 Members of the Welsh Assembly elected using a *hybrid electoral system*, with 40 elected in *single-member constituencies* and 20 elected in five *multi-member constituencies* from *party lists* to ensure a greater degree of *proportionality*. The voter may cast two votes, one for a candidate in a single-member constituency and one for a party list in a multi-member constituency.

member states (EU): countries which — having joined the *European Union* by signing a treaty of accession (originally the 1957 Treaty of Rome) — participate in EU decision-making and are bound by its laws.

- There are currently 15 EU member states (Austria, Belgium, Denmark, Finland, France, Germany, Greece, Ireland, Italy, Luxembourg, Netherlands, Portugal, Spain, Sweden and the UK) and several more hoping to join (such as Poland and Hungary).

MEP: see *Member of the European Parliament.*

metropolitan district council: an elected *local government* assembly with responsibilities for city planning, roads and traffic, housing, refuse collection, education, and leisure and recreation.

- Metropolitan *councillors* are elected every 4 years.
- *e.g.* Manchester City Council.

middle class: the socioeconomic category largely made up of professional, managerial and administrative employees and their families. See also *social class, class alignment* and *class voting.*

Millbank/Millbank Tower: the building by the Thames in London where the national headquarters of the *Labour Party* have been located since 1997.

- The word Millbank has become synonymous with Labour's leadership and strategy.

minister: a member of the government with specific responsibilities within a *department.*

- In addition to *cabinet ministers* there are three ranks of *junior minister: ministers of state, parliamentary under-secretaries,* and *parliamentary secretaries.*
- *e.g.* In the *Home Office* there are several ministers including the *home secretary* (a cabinet minister) and a junior minister who is responsible for prisons.

Ministerial Code: the document setting out the duties and responsibilities of a government *minister,* including a section on *collective responsibility.*

- Prior to 1997, the code was known as *Questions of Procedure for Ministers.*

ministerial responsibility: a *convention* of the *constitution* that outlines the duties expected of a *minister* in the government.

- There are two aspects of ministerial responsibility. See *individual* and *collective responsibility.*

minister of state: one of the three ranks of junior minister.

ministry: a part of the *civil service* that is responsible for the formulation and administration of a particular aspect of government *policy* which is staffed by *civil servants* and headed by a *cabinet minister*.

■ *e.g.* Ministry of Defence.

■ *TIP* Note that, as well as ministries, some parts of the civil service are known as *offices* (e.g. Northern Ireland) and others as *departments* (e.g. Environment, Food and Rural Affairs).

minority government: a government formed by a *political party* without an *overall majority* of MPs in the *House of Commons*.

● Because of the lack of a majority over all the other parties in the House of Commons and the possibility of a united opposition, a minority government is less able to control the passage of its *legislation* and is less stable (due to its susceptibility to a *vote of confidence*).

■ *e.g.* From November 1976 (when it lost a *by-election* in Walsall North), the Labour government was a minority government. Technically, the Conservative government between November 1994 and April 1995 became a minority government when the *whip* was withdrawn from eight Conservative *euro-sceptic* MPs (and they were joined by a ninth who declined the *whip*).

minor party: a *political party* with few (if any) *representatives* in elected positions, limited membership and which attracts a small share of the vote at elections in which it fields *candidates*.

■ *e.g.* The *Socialist Labour Party*.

monarch: a *head of state* whose claim to political *power* is based on the hereditary principle rather than *democratic election*.

● In practice in the UK, the monarch has little political power but acts always on the advice of the *prime minister*. The monarch's *prerogative powers*, such as the right to call a *general election*, are in reality exercised by the prime minister.

monarchy: a political system in which the *head of state* is a *monarch*.

● The UK is described more accurately as a constitutional monarchy due to the constitutional arrangements that place restrictions on the exercise of political power by the king or queen.

money bill: proposed *legislation* certified by the *speaker* as dealing exclusively with money. See the reduction on the power of delay in the *Parliament Act (1911)*.

■ *e.g.* An example is the *Budget*, over which the *House of Lords* has reduced influence.

MP: see *Member of Parliament*.

MSP: see *Member of the Scottish Parliament*.

multi-member constituency: a geographical area represented by more than one elected official.

■ *e.g.* Some *electoral systems* (such as the *single transferable vote* in *European elections* in Northern Ireland and the *hybrid electoral systems* for the *Scottish Parliament* and the *Welsh Assembly*) make use of multi-member constituencies to ensure a greater degree of *proportionality*. For instance, in European elections Northern Ireland is treated as one *constituency* that elects three *Members of the European Parliament*.

■ *TIP* Multi-member constituencies may be contrasted with the *single-member constituencies* represented by MPs at *Westminster*.

multi-party system: a political system in which more than two *political parties* exist and contest elections with a realistic prospect of achieving political power.

● Responsibility for forming the government either changes between parties from one election to another or is shared in a *coalition*.

■ *e.g.* Under its *proportional electoral system* after 1945, Italy experienced a succession of multi-party coalition governments.

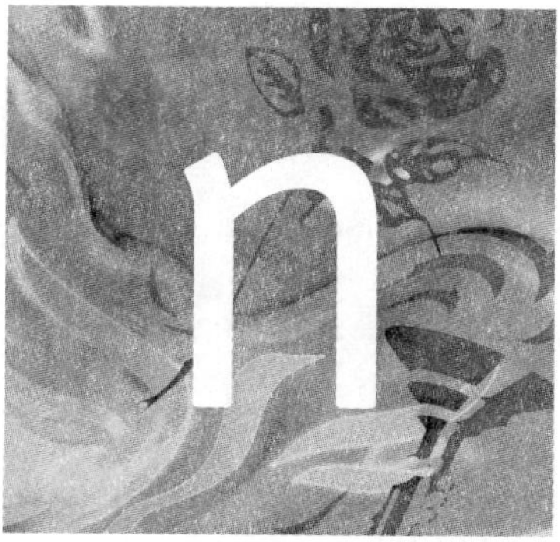

National Assembly for Wales: see *Welsh Assembly.*

National Economic Development Council (NEDC): a *corporatist* forum that met from 1961 to 1993, where government *ministers, civil servants,* employers and *trade union* officials discussed economic *policy.*

National Executive Committee (NEC): the administrative authority of the *Labour Party,* established under Clause VIII of the party's *constitution,* with responsibility for ensuring the smooth running of the party machine and overseeing the party work between *conferences.*

- The NEC's membership (currently 32) reflects that of the wider party and includes *representatives* from the *trade unions, affiliated* socialist organisations, the party's MPs and MEPs and the party leadership. Conference elects 24 of the NEC's members.
- The NEC's roles include helping in policy-making, disciplining Labour Party members, looking after party finances and playing a part in the selection of parliamentary *candidates.*

TIP In the past, the NEC has often disagreed with the party leadership, but in recent years the majority of the NEC's members (partly as a result of changes in the membership structure) have been more loyal to the leadership.

National Farmers' Union (NFU): a *pressure group,* representing the interests of the UK's farmers, which — through regular consultation with *civil servants* and *ministers* — enjoys *insider group* status.

National Front: the extreme *right-wing political party* that was founded in 1967, split in the 1980s and from where the *British National Party* emerged.

nationalisation: a transfer of an economic enterprise from private to public (state) ownership and control.

- Nationalisation is associated with *socialist ideology.*
- The original *Clause IV* in the *Labour Party*'s *constitution* of 1918 contained a commitment to nationalisation. Clause IV was rewritten in 1995.

e.g. After the Second World War, the railways were nationalised and taken into public ownership as British Rail. In the 1990s, *John Major*'s government privatised British Rail and trains are now operated by a number of separate, privately owned companies.

nationalism: a patriotic belief in one's country's national independence and self-determination.

■ *e.g.* The nationalist parties in Scotland and Wales are, respectively, the *Scottish National Party* and *Plaid Cymru*.

National Policy Forum (Labour Party): the *Labour Party* body, established in 1990, with responsibilities in the party's policy-making process.

● The National Policy Forum appoints commissions, with around 20 members and headed by a *frontbench MP*, which produce reports on a specific *policy* area for *conference*, via the *National Executive Committee*, to approve.

■ *TIP* The National Policy Forum has contributed to the declining importance of the Labour Party conference. Following procedural changes in 1997, conference may now only consider policy proposals previously considered by National Policy Forum commissions. This has reduced conference's role to approving or rejecting these commissions' proposals and has increased the leadership's control over policy-making.

● The *Conservative Party* also has a *Policy Forum*.

Natural Law Party: a *minor party* which has semi-religious views and *policies*, including the use of transcendental meditation.

NEC: see *National Executive Committee*.

NEDC: see *National Economic Development Council*.

negative campaigning: an electioneering technique to depress the opposition's electoral support by attacking a *political party* or *candidate* rather than promoting the campaigning party's own attributes.

● Negative campaigning and attack advertisements are widely used in US elections and are becoming increasingly common in UK elections.

■ *e.g.* In the 2001 *general election* the *Conservative Party* sought to draw the voters' attention to what it regarded as a failing in government *policy*. In a *party election broadcast,* Labour's Early Release Scheme was blamed for a number of drug offences and cases of rape.

Neill Report: published in October 1998, this report made a number of recommendations on election expenditure and the funding of *political parties* which the government incorporated in the *Queen's Speech* in November 1999.

● The report's author was Lord Neill, who succeeded Lord Nolan as chairman of the *Committee on Standards in Public Life* (set up by *John Major* after the *cash for questions* scandal in 1994).

● The report's main recommendations were a ban on foreign donations, the requirement for publication of all donations over £5,000 nationally and £1,000 locally, that company shareholders be balloted over corporate donations and sponsorship, a £20 million cap on party spending at *general elections*, the introduction of controls on spending in *referendums* (including equal state funding for yes and no campaigns), the establishment of an electoral commission for registering parties and checking finances, an increase in state funding for *opposition parties* in *parliament*, the creation of a Policy Development Fund and a cap at 100 on the number of *special advisers* appointed by the party in government.

neo-liberalism: the dominant Western political *ideology* founded on beliefs in individual *rights*, limiting the powers of government and free market economics.

New Labour: a term used by *Tony Blair* for the first time at the 1994 *Labour Party conference* to describe the modernised Labour Party as distinct from *Old Labour*.

- The modernisation of the party into New Labour can be traced back to the election of *Neil Kinnock* as leader following the heavy defeat at the 1983 *general election*.

- New Labour characteristics are a more leader-dominated party (with correspondingly less power for the *trade unions* and *Constituency Labour Parties* with the introduction of *one member, one vote*), the re-drafted *Clause IV* of the party's *constitution* and the abandonment of the historic commitment to *nationalisation*, and the repositioning of the party's policies to attract *middle-class* voters.

new magistracy: the trend since 1979 of delegating functions of government — including the spending of public money — to non-elected (and less accountable) bodies such as *quangos*.

New Right: the political *ideology* (closely associated with *neo-liberalism*) which emphasises individual freedom, law and order, and free market economics to promote economic growth.

- The ideology developed in the UK and the USA in the 1970s which has become synonymous with *Thatcherism*.

new urban left: the political movement associated with *socialist* Labour-controlled *local councils* in the 1980s.

new working class: a division of the *working class* which includes people who typically live in the south, own their own homes, are employed in the private sector and are not members of *trade unions*.

- The distinction between the traditional and new working class was identified by Ivor Crewe in the 1980s to explain declining support for the *Labour Party* and an increased share of the vote for the *Conservative Party* amongst manual workers.

Next Steps agency: see *executive agency*.

Next Steps Report: see *Ibbs Report*.

NFU: see *National Farmers' Union*.

1922 Committee: comprises all Conservative *backbench* MPs and seeks to communicate their views to the party leadership.

- The committee elects an executive committee and chair. The chair is responsible for organising party leadership elections.

no-confidence motion: a *debate* in the *House of Commons* usually only called for by the *opposition* when the government's *majority* is small and its defeat in a vote is therefore possible.

- The loss of a no-confidence vote obliges a government to resign or call a *general election*.

- There is debate over the *convention* of a government being obliged to resign when it is defeated in an important vote in the House of Commons and whether such a defeat should be treated as a vote of no-confidence. In 1994, for example, the government refused to resign following a defeat in the House of Commons on increasing VAT on domestic fuel because it did not recognise the vote as a no-confidence motion.

- *e.g.* No-confidence votes are rare and a government was only defeated once in this way during the twentieth century (James Callaghan's Labour government in March 1979).

- *TIP* When working with a small majority, a government may tell its *back-benchers* that it is treating a vote as a vote of no-confidence in order to ensure their loyalty and to delay a general election. In 1994, for example, *John Major* announced that he would consider a vote on increased contributions to the *European Union* as a confidence motion.

Nolan Committee: the alternative name for the *Committee on Standards in Public Life*, established by *John Major* following the *cash for questions* scandal in 1994 and chaired by Lord Nolan.

Nolan Report: the 1995 report and recommendations published by the *Committee on Standards in Public Life* (the *Nolan Committee*).

- In response to the *cash for questions* scandal, the Nolan Report recommended a ban on paid advocacy by MPs, disclosure by MPs (in the *Register of Members' Interests*) of any outside income received because of MP-status, the establishment of a code of conduct for MPs and the appointment of a *parliamentary commissioner for standards.*

non-departmental public body: an alternative name for *quango.*

non-departmental select committees: parliamentary bodies that examine public policy and administration via *scrutiny* of the *executive* and aspects of the *legislature*'s work.

- These committees do not scrutinise the work of specific government *departments. Departmental select committees* perform this role.

- Non-departmental select committees may be permanent or ad hoc. They take oral and written evidence and publish reports.

- *e.g.* Such committees include the *Public Accounts Committee*, the *Select Committee on European Legislation*, the *Select Committee on Standards and Privileges* and the *Committee on Standards in Public Life.*

- *TIP* Be able to distinguish between non-departmental and departmental select committees and distinguish both from *standing committees.*

non-money bill: proposed *legislation* not defined as a *money bill*. See also *Parliament Act (1911)* and *Parliament Act (1949).*

non-partisan: an adjective denoting the absence of influence from or bias towards a *political party.*

- *e.g. Select committees* of the *House of Commons* are supposed to carry out their *scrutiny* of the government in a non-partisan manner.

non-voter: someone who, although entitled to, does not vote.

● Falling *turnout* levels in UK elections indicate increasing numbers of non-voters. This has been explained by apathy amongst the *electorate*, attributed to disillusionment with the *political parties* and *candidates* and, more widely, with electoral and political processes in general.

Northcote-Trevelyan Report (1854): the *civil service* reform that recommended the abolition of patronage and nepotism and created a meritocratic and neutral government bureaucracy with entry through open, competitive examination.

Northern Ireland Assembly: the elected *legislature* created in the 1998 *Good Friday Agreement* to meet at Stormont Castle in Belfast and exercise devolved administrative powers in areas such as agriculture, education and the environment (see *devolution*).

No Turning Back Group: the faction within the *Conservative Party* which *right-wing* MPs established in the 1980s to promote *Thatcherite* policies.

Number 10: the *Prime Minister's Office* at 10 *Downing Street*, London.

occupational class: the categorisation of social and economic *class* according to employment.

▨ *e.g.* The *working class* is defined as those who earn their living from manual jobs, whereas the professional class includes doctors and lawyers.

office: a part of the *civil service* responsible for formulating and administering a particular aspect of government *policy*, and staffed by *civil servants* who are headed by a *cabinet minister*.

▨ *e.g.* Home Office.

▨ *TIP* Note that some parts of the civil service are known as *ministries* (e.g. Defence) and others as *departments* (e.g. Environment, Food and Rural Affairs).

official committees: complementary to *cabinet committees*, these committees are composed entirely of *civil servants* who often meet in advance to prepare for ministerial meetings.

Old Labour: as distinct from *New Labour*, the term is used to describe a historic association with the *working class*, the *trade unions* and a commitment to *socialist* principles, in particular *nationalisation* as embodied in the *Labour Party constitution*'s old *Clause IV*.

● The transformation from Old to New Labour took place from 1983 under the party leaderships of *Neil Kinnock*, *John Smith* and *Tony Blair*.

ombudsman: the alternative name for the parliamentary commissioner for administration, established in 1967 to investigate complaints of maladministration against central government *departments*.

● A member of the public can only refer a complaint to the ombudsman through an MP, and the matter is only investigated when there is no other form of redress.

● Ombudsmen also exist in other areas: for example, the health service, the prison service and for housing association tenants.

OMOV: see *one member, one vote*.

one-line whip: the instruction from the *party whips* to MPs indicating that attendance is requested at the *House of Commons* for a particular vote.

● Weekly instructions are issued to a party's MPs from the *whips' office*. More important votes are accompanied by *two* and *three-line whips*.

one member, one vote (OMOV): a feature of *Labour Party* decision-making adopted during the party's modernisation in 1993 and which has, in most situations, signalled the end of the *block vote*.

- OMOV is regarded as more democratic and is used at the party *conference*, in leadership elections and in the selection of parliamentary *candidates*.
- *William Hague* embraced the OMOV principle to change the way *Conservative Party* leaders are elected.

one-nation conservatism: an expression associated with the nineteenth-century Conservative *prime minister* Benjamin Disraeli and describing the *ideology* that deplores the division between rich and poor and which promotes inclusiveness. See also *Tory*.

- One-nation conservatism retains *Conservative Party* adherents who believe in government intervention and the promotion of full employment. Its main opposition in the party is from the *New Right Thatcherites*.

open government: a system of government that allows the public and *media* relatively free access to information held by government.

- The campaign for open government in the UK has involved *pressure group* activity promoting a Freedom of Information Act (see *freedom of information*).

open list: a feature of an *electoral system* in which voters can express a preference either for a party's list of *candidates* or for a particular candidate whose name appears on the list.

- Open lists allow for *proportional representation* and can form part of a *hybrid electoral system* such as *AV plus*.

opinion poll: a survey of the views of a *sample* of the voting public (usually between 1,000 and 2,000 randomly chosen voters) to assess the state of *public opinion* and the likely voting intentions of the *electorate*.

- Polling organisations such as NOP, Harris, MORI, Gallup and ICM claim to be able to predict the *political parties'* share of the vote at *general elections* to within 3% in 95% of cases.
- At the 1992 general election, much attention was paid to opinion polls, but their failure to predict the result accurately increased scepticism about polling organisations' ability to forecast. The *Labour Party's* average lead on polling day was forecast at 0.9%. The *Conservative Party*, however, won by 7.6% — a record error of 8.5%. Readjustments have since been made to take account of the apparent reluctance of Conservative voters to admit their allegiance — the so-called 'spiral of silence'.
- At the 1997 general election, opinion polls were much more accurate, but many still overstated Labour's share of the vote and its lead. According to Ivor Crewe, the mean error of 2% in the final polls was the third largest since 1945.
- At the 2001 *general election*, the polls were again inaccurate. In the final *campaign* polls, NOP in **The Sunday Times** had a 17% lead for Labour, as did Gallup in the **Daily Telegraph**. In **The Times**, MORI had a 15% lead. ICM, in the

Guardian, came closest with an 11% lead. The actual result was a Labour victory by 9%.

■ *TIP* Opinion polls are also useful for providing information on voters' perceptions of leaders, party images and *policy* preferences. They allow shifts in public opinion to be tracked.

opposition: the *political party* with the second largest number of MPs in the *House of Commons*.

● The opposition is sometimes referred to as the official opposition or, more correctly, Her Majesty's Loyal Opposition. The most senior figures in the opposition make up the *shadow cabinet*. The *leader of the opposition* receives a salary in addition to that earned as an MP.

● The relationship between government and opposition is not always antagonistic. The government seeks cooperation in areas such as the administration of *parliament* and the staffing of *select* and *standing committees*.

● The opposition is allocated a certain amount of time (*opposition days*) in the House of Commons during which it may choose the topic of *debate*.

■ *TIP* All those parties represented in the House of Commons, though not in the government, may be referred to as opposition parties.

opposition days: the 20 days in a *parliamentary session* during which the topics for *debate* in the *House of Commons* are chosen by the *opposition*.

Order in Council: a government directive, with the force of law, issued through the *Privy Council*.

● The government may use such orders when *parliament* is not in session and when *legislation* may therefore not be passed in the normal manner. Orders may be issued in times of emergency. An example was during the fuel crisis in autumn 2000, when supplies of fuel to essential services needed to be guaranteed.

● Orders in Council are a written source of the *constitution*.

Osmotherley Rules: named after the *civil servant* Edward Osmotherley, these rules limit the type of questions that parliamentary committees are allowed to ask civil servants.

● They state that committees must not ask civil servants 'questions in the field of political controversy'. They also seek to preserve the anonymity of civil servants by not allowing questions to be asked about individual civil servants or the advice they have given to *ministers*.

● The Osmotherley Rules are often regarded as a shield used by civil servants and an obstacle to effective parliamentary *scrutiny*.

Oughton Report (1993): named after the leader of the *Cabinet Office* Efficiency Unit, Sir John Oughton, the report made recommendations regarding better training, wider recruitment and more flexible terms of employment in the *civil service*.

outsider group: a type of *pressure group* that is not regularly consulted by the *ministers* and *civil servants* who make *policy* in the area in which it has an interest and which, therefore, uses other methods to gain influence.

- The academic Wyn Grant distinguishes between outsider and *insider groups* on the basis of whether or not they enjoy access to government decision-makers. He recognises that not all outsider groups seek insider status and draws the distinction between 'potential insiders' (e.g. the *Institute for Public Policy Research* when the *Labour Party* was in *opposition* before 1997), 'outsider groups by necessity' (e.g. the Campaign for Nuclear Disarmament, whose unilateralist view is not supported by any of the main parties) and 'ideological outsider groups' (e.g. the radical environmental group Earth First).

- **e.g.** Earth First and animal liberation pressure groups are examples of outsider groups that use extra-parliamentary methods to seek to achieve their aims.

- **TIP** The key distinction to note is between outsider and insider groups.

overall majority: the difference, expressed in terms of votes (although rarely used for an individual *candidate* in a single *constituency*) or, more commonly, *seats* in the *House of Commons* (for a *political party* after a *general election*), between the winning candidate or party and the rest added together, which describes the extent of the victory resulting from an election.

- A *hung parliament* (e.g. the result of the February 1974 general election) is one in which no one party has an overall majority of MPs in the House of Commons.

- **e.g.** After the 2001 general election, the Labour government held an overall majority of 167 *seats* in the House of Commons, meaning that the party had 167 more MPs than all the other parties added together.

pairing: the arrangement reached between *party whips* for MPs from the *government* and *opposition* sides to be matched so that the absence of one MP at a vote in the *House of Commons* is cancelled out by the absence of the other. See also *two-line whip*.

Palace of Westminster: the building in central London containing the debating chambers and committee rooms of the *House of Commons* and the *House of Lords*.

parliament: an institution of *government*, comprising *representatives* elected by voters, whose functions are to debate, scrutinise and pass *legislation*.

- In the UK the *Westminster* Parliament comprises the *Houses of Commons* and *Lords* and, strictly, the *monarch*. Together, these bodies fulfil the function of the *legislature*.
- As a result of *devolution*, there is now a *Scottish Parliament* in Edinburgh. Less powerful assemblies have also been established for Wales and Northern Ireland.
- *TIP* The word is alternatively used to mean the period of time between *general elections*, the maximum length of which is 5 years.

Parliament Act (1911): the *statute* that confirmed the subordinate role of the *House of Lords* to the *House of Commons*.

- The main provisions of the act were to reduce the legislative power of the *House of Lords* from *veto* to delay. *Non-money bills* could be delayed by no more than two *parliamentary sessions* and *money bills* (those certified by the *speaker* as dealing exclusively with money) would pass into law 1 month after leaving the Commons, with or without the approval of the Lords. Under the act, the House of Lords retained its power to veto a proposal to extend the life of a *parliament* by the *House of Commons*.

Parliament Act (1949): the *statute* that further subordinated the legislative power of the *House of Lords* to the *House of Commons*, initiated by the *Parliament Act (1911)*, by reducing the delaying power over *non-money bills* to one *parliamentary session*.

parliamentary candidate: a person seeking election to the *House of Commons* as the choice of the voters in a *constituency* in either a *by-election* or a *general election*.

- A parliamentary candidate must be at least 21 years old and a *citizen* of the UK, another Commonwealth country or the Republic of Ireland. A candidate must be nominated by ten *registered voters* from the constituency and must put down a *deposit* of £500 (which is returned to a candidate who receives 5% or more of the votes cast).

- Those disqualified from standing for election include undischarged bankrupts, members of the *House of Lords*, judges and *civil servants*.
- In the main *political parties*, there are established procedures for the selection of parliamentary candidates.

parliamentary commissioner for administration: see *ombudsman*.

parliamentary commissioner for standards: established as a result of the *Nolan Report*, and working with the *Select Committee on Standards and Privileges*, to scrutinise the conduct and interests of MPs and to supervise the compilation and maintenance of the *Register of Members' Interests*.

- MPs may refer to the parliamentary commissioner for standards to seek clarification on the acceptability of certain interests and on what should be included in the Register of Members' Interests.

parliamentary government: a system of government centred on a *parliament* of which the *head of government* is a member. See also *parliamentary sovereignty* and *presidential government*.

- *e.g.* In theory, the UK has a system of parliamentary government but in practice, parliament is not the most important institution of government because of the dominance of the *legislature* by the *executive*.

Parliamentary Labour Party (PLP): the body comprising all *Labour Party* MPs.

- The PLP elects a chairperson whose role is to liaise with the party leader.
- Members of the PLP elect the party's *shadow cabinet* when in *opposition*. Together with the party's *Members of the European Parliament*, the PLP controls one-third of the votes in the *electoral college* for the election of leader and deputy leader.

parliamentary private secretary (PPS): an MP who acts as an assistant to a *minister*, providing advice and a two-way link between the *minister* and *backbenchers*.

- Ministers appoint their own PPS with the *prime minister*'s approval. Though an unpaid position, it is sought after as a route to higher office.
- *TIP* Traditionally, only senior ministers had a PPS, but in recent years their number has increased, with *junior ministers* now also routinely appointing PPSs. This has significantly increased the *payroll vote*: that is, those MPs whose loyalty can be expected due to their holding a position from which they can be dismissed.

parliamentary questions: MPs' oral questions put to government *ministers*, including the *prime minister*, on one afternoon each week, at a time set aside for this purpose. See also *written questions*.

- Through parliamentary questions MPs may gain little information that might not be more effectively sought by other means (such as written questions). The intention of the questioner is often to attract publicity to a particular issue, to impress *constituents* or influential figures in the party, or to embarrass the government.

parliamentary secretary: one of the three ranks of *junior minister*.

parliamentary session: the division of time in a *parliament* — lasting approximately a year and usually beginning in November with the *Queen's Speech* — during which *legislation* must be concluded because of its carrying forward being restricted.

parliamentary sovereignty: a central doctrine of the UK *constitution* which states that *parliament* is the supreme law-making body in the country.

- The doctrine distinguishes the UK's constitutional arrangements from those of other countries. For instance, it limits the scope of *judicial review* because parliament's ability to pass any law it chooses cannot be restricted by the courts.
- There are limitations to this doctrine, however, notably due to the government's dominance of the *House of Commons*.
- Parliamentary sovereignty has also been undermined by the UK's international obligations, particularly its membership of the *European Union* and the supremacy of EU law over *acts of parliament*. The passage of the *Human Rights Act* in 2000 also has implications for parliamentary sovereignty.

parliamentary under-secretary: one of the three ranks of *junior minister*.

partisan: the influence of *political party*, used particularly to describe bias.

- *e.g.* A committee of the *House of Commons* might be described as partisan if its members were under the influence of *party whips* or if it displayed bias towards the interests of one party over another.

partisan alignment: the long-term psychological attachment developed by voters to a *political party*. Also known as party identification or *partisanship*.

- Partisan alignment can determine *voting behaviour* over and above a voting preference based on a rational assessment of a party's aims, promises or practices.
- Although a significant proportion of the voting public still displays partisan alignment, this phenomenon was more visible in the UK *electorate* before the 1970s and is associated with stability and predictability in voting behaviour.
- There is a link between partisan alignment and *class alignment*.

partisan dealignment: also known as party dealignment, this describes the drop in the number of voters displaying a strong and lasting identification with the main *political parties*.

- Evidence for partisan dealignment can be seen in the increase in votes for the *Liberal Democrats* and *nationalist* parties, and the willingness of voters to register *protest votes*, particularly at *by-elections*.
- Party dealignment seemed to have been at least halted in 1992, when increasing numbers claimed 'very strong' or 'fairly strong' identification with political parties. In 1997, however, the decline in the share of the vote for the *Conservative Party* again prompted observers to support this theory's continued relevance.
- The causes of party dealignment are argued to be both an increase in the importance of *short-term factors* as well as *class dealignment* (that is, party attachments based on the class–party tie). *Rational choice* voting has increased with greater levels of education and access to information through the *media*.

There is also evidence of increased cynicism and disillusionment with the main parties, as a result of scandal and failure to fulfil promises.

■ *TIP* There is a debate about whether increased electoral *volatility* has been caused by party dealignment or whether it has merely accompanied it.

partisanship: evidence for the influence of or bias shown towards a *political party*.

● The term can be used in the same sense as partisan alignment.

party: see *political party*.

party activist: a member of a *political party* who participates in its functions and procedures.

● Party activists are often more extreme than and therefore unrepresentative of both ordinary *party members* and those who vote for the party.

party chairman (Conservative Party): the party official whom the party leader appoints to run *Central Office*, with responsibility for national election *campaigns* and the party's organisation and structure.

● The current *Conservative Party* chairman is David Davis.

● The *Labour Party* also has a chairman (Charles Clarke) who has had a seat in the *cabinet* since 2001.

party conference: see *conference*.

party discipline: the loyalty and behaviour expected of MPs in following their party's official position on *policy* issues, particularly when voting in the *House of Commons*.

● As well as for reasons of natural political inclination, party discipline is usually displayed by an MP partly because an obligation is felt to the voters, partly due to a desire to achieve advancement and partly because of the threat of sanctions from the *party whips*.

party election broadcast: a television or radio advertisement transmitted during an election *campaign* in airtime allocated free to *political parties* by broadcasters due to the prohibition on paying for such airtime in the Broadcasting Act.

● The number of party political broadcasts allowed to each party is strictly regulated and determined by a combination of the number of *candidates* the party is fielding and the party's representation in the previous *parliament*. In recent *general elections,* the *Conservative* and *Labour Parties* have been allowed five broadcasts each and the *Liberal Democrats* four.

■ *TIP* The limited number of television and radio advertisements in the UK may be contrasted with the situation in the USA, where parties and candidates can purchase airtime. This helps to explain why the broadcast *media* are said to have less of an impact on the results of elections in the UK.

party identifier: see *identifier*.

party list system: an *electoral system* in which voters choose between *political parties*, each of which publishes a list containing the same number of *candidates* as *representatives* to be elected in a particular area.

● This system features *proportional representation* as each party is allocated a share of the representatives to be elected in proportion to the share of the votes cast for the party.

■ *e.g.* A *closed-list* system was introduced in the UK in the 1999 *European elections*.

■ *TIP* Be able to distinguish between the closed-list system, where the voter is required to vote for a political party rather than a candidate, and the *open-list* system, which forms a part of *AV plus*, where the voter can vote either for a political party or for a candidate from one of the party lists.

party member: a person belonging to a *political party*, usually by paying an annual subscription which — depending on the party — entitles that person to participate in certain aspects of decision-making such as selecting *parliamentary candidates*, electing the leader and deciding on *policy*. See also *party activist*.

party political broadcast: the same as a *party election broadcast* but it is transmitted at times other than during election *campaigns*.

party system: the nature of competition between *political parties*.

● Debate surrounds the most fitting description for the UK's party system. The types of system identified in different countries at different times are the *single-party system*, the *dominant-party system*, the *two-party system* and the *multi-party system*.

party voter: a voter who demonstrates a long-term and consistent inclination to vote for a particular *political party*. See also *alignment*.

● During periods of *alignment*, when a large proportion of the *electorate* are party voters, there is a tendency towards stability and predictability of election results. Since the 1950s, there has been a decline in the number of party voters and a higher degree of electoral *volatility*.

● Broad generalisations can be made about certain characteristics shared by party voters. For example, stereotypical Conservative voters are *middle class*, live in the south of England and own their own homes. In recent years, Labour voters have become more difficult to stereotype, although traditionally they have been *working class*, have lived in the north of England, Scotland or Wales and have been more likely to live in council houses.

party whip: a member of either the *House of Commons* or the *House of Lords* with responsibility within the party for parliamentary business, in particular ensuring MPs' attendance to vote and maintaining *party discipline*.

● The party whips work in the *whips' office* and report to the party's *chief whip*. They issue weekly instructions to the party's MPs informing them of when they are required to attend and vote in the House of Commons.

● In the House of Lords, party discipline is less strict and the whips play a reduced role.

● MPs are usually keen to find favour with their party whips as they are able to influence advancement in the party. Party whips are also able to apply sanctions.

● Serving as a party whip is often regarded as a route to higher office.

patronage: the power of appointment which, in constitutional practice, rests largely with the *prime minister*.

- The prime minister exercises the power of patronage on behalf of the *monarch* in appointing *cabinet* and other *ministers*, members of the *House of Lords* and chairs of *royal commissions*.
- Critics of prime ministerial power point out the unchecked nature of patronage in the UK compared, for example, to the USA, where many presidential appointments are subject to confirmation by the Senate.

payroll vote: the votes cast in the *House of Commons* upon which the governing party can most confidently rely because the MPs who vote are employed by the government and are therefore strictly bound by *party discipline*.

- *e.g.* Cabinet and *junior ministers* are part of the payroll vote. So too are *parliamentary private secretaries*, even though they do not draw a government salary in addition to that earned as an MP.

peak association: an umbrella group that represents a number of *pressure groups* with similar interests.

- *e.g.* The *Trades Union Congress* represents many different *trade unions* and the *Confederation of British Industry* speaks on behalf of a number of separate companies or employers.

peer: a member of the *House of Lords*.

- There are several types of peer (e.g. duke, marquis, earl, viscount, baron). The appointment of *life peers* was provided for in the *Life Peerages Act (1958)*. Since the passage of this act, very few new *hereditary peers* have been created, and in 1999 all but 92 of their number lost their rights to sit and vote in the House of Lords.

Performance and Innovation Unit: established in 1998 as part of the *Cabinet Office* with the aim of improving the delivery of *policies* and services that involve more than one government *department*.

- The Performance and Innovation Unit and the *Social Exclusion Unit* are regarded as key elements in providing the coordination of government departments which the Labour government calls 'joined-up government'.

permanent secretary: the highest rank of *civil servant* in charge of a government *department* and reporting to the responsible *cabinet minister*.

- The *prime minister* has the power to appoint permanent secretaries.

personal responsibility: an aspect of the constitutional *convention* of *individual responsibility* which emphasises a *minister's* duty to be answerable for the conduct of his or her private life, whether or not this affects the ability to perform as a government minister.

- *e.g.* Ron Davies resigned as Welsh secretary in 1998 following his mysterious 'moment of madness' on Clapham Common.

petition: a collection of petitioners' signatures requesting government action.

- Petitions show public support for a cause and are used to attract publicity.

Plaid Cymru: the Welsh *nationalist* party which aims to protect the Welsh language and culture, and is represented in the *House of Commons* and the *Welsh Assembly*.

PLP: see *Parliamentary Labour Party*.

pluralism: a system of government that allows and encourages public partici-pation, particularly through the activities of *pressure groups* seeking to influence government.

- The UK is often described as a pluralist society because of the activities of competing pressure groups, with the government acting as referee. Pluralism, however, is also regarded by some as an ideal that is not reached in the UK because of the inequality of access and influence amongst competing groups.

policy: a course of action formulated and promised by a *political party* for imple-mentation when in government.

- Party leaders are often keen to emphasise the procedures for ordinary *party members* to participate in policy-making. However, policy-making in most parties is centralised around the leadership.
- At a *general election,* a party presents its policy commitments to the *electorate* in a *manifesto.*

Policy Forum: the *Conservative Party* body created in the 1998 **Fresh Future** restruc-turing whereby ordinary *party members*, MPs and *policy* experts meet in regional congresses that have advisory powers and can make policy proposals to *conference.*

- The *Labour Party* has a *National Policy Forum.*

policy network: *policy* formulation by a combination of the government and a community of regularly consulted *pressure groups.*

- *e.g.* A wide variety of agricultural, environmental and consumer groups influence decisions on food policy at the Department for the Environment, Food and Rural Affairs.
- *TIP* The academic R. Baggott distinguishes between policy communities and issue networks. The latter have more groups participating, the relations between members tend towards instability, there is less likelihood of consensus, and relationships with the government are less close and not continuous.

Policy Unit: created in 1974 as part of the *Prime Minister's Office* to provide medium to long-term *policy* advice to the *prime minister.*

- The Policy Unit comprises political appointees taken on as temporary *civil servants* and permanent civil servants on secondment from other government *departments*. It provides policy initiatives that may be drawn from a variety of sources, including *think tanks* and other countries.
- The Policy Unit has become increasingly influential in recent years and particu-larly since 1997.

political adviser: see *adviser.*

political levy: the sum paid to the *Labour Party* by an *affiliated* organisation, such as a *trade union*, in order to enroll its members as affiliated party members. See also *levy plus.*

- Payment of political levy grants voting rights to affiliated organisations and their members at the annual *conference*. This has raised concerns about affiliated organisations, particularly trade unions, being able to buy votes. See also *block vote.*

political party: an organisation whose members share a common *ideology* and *policy* positions, and whose purpose is to participate in government through securing the election of its *candidates* to the *legislature* and, possibly, the *executive*.

Political Unit (No. 10): formerly known as the Political Office, this part of the *Prime Minister's Office* assists the *prime minister* in liaising with the party.

- Unlike the other parts of the Prime Minister's Office, the Political Unit is funded by the party rather than by the taxpayer.

politician: in the broadest sense, a person engaged in politics.

- To define the word more narrowly, the qualification of running for election is what distinguishes a politician from, say, a *civil servant*. In this sense, the distinction between politics and *government* might also be drawn.

poll: the recorded result of an election or the counting of votes at an election. See also *opinion poll*.

polling card: a card that identifies a *registered voter* and which is presented at the *polling station* in exchange for a *ballot paper*.

- Polling cards are posted in advance of elections to those entitled to vote and provide details of the date of the election and the closest place where a vote may be cast.

polling day: the day on which an election takes place.

- The polling day for a *general election* is the choice of the *prime minister* and this is regarded as a considerable political advantage.

polling station: the venue where votes are cast at an election, usually in a building used by the local community such as a school or church hall.

- In a parliamentary election, a number of locations convenient for population centres are used as polling stations, with voters being advised of the closest polling station to where they live on their *polling card*.
- In recent elections, alternative and even more accessible polling stations, such as supermarkets, have been tested in an effort to increase *turnout*. These experiments, however, have proved largely unsuccessful.

pollster: a person who compiles and analyses *opinion polls*.

post-modern election campaign: a style of *campaign* with central coordination of targeted *constituencies*, *media* management and the use of *opinion polls*, *focus groups* and advertising consultants.

- *e.g.* The *Labour Party*'s 1997 *general election* campaign is considered the prime example.

postwar consensus: the broad agreement between the *Labour* and *Conservative Parties* over domestic and foreign *policy* after the Second World War.

- Amongst the fundamentals on which the parties agreed were the need for the *welfare state*, the pursuit of Keynesian economic policy, membership of NATO and the granting of independence to overseas colonies.
- *TIP* By the 1970s, the postwar consensus was considered to have disappeared. After *Margaret Thatcher*'s demise and the rise of *New Labour*, some commentators said a new consensus had emerged.

power (political): the ability to make others do what they otherwise would not have done (through membership and control of government institutions).

- In a *democracy*, political power is won through victory in elections, whereas in other systems it is often gained and retained through the use or threat of violence.

- *e.g.* A *political party* is described as being in power when it has formed a government by virtue of being the *majority party* in the *House of Commons*.

PPS: see *parliamentary private secretary*.

PR: see *proportional representation*.

pre-modern election campaign: a style of *campaign* with local *canvassing*, local public meetings and the use of low-budget *media* such as posters and pamphlets.

- *e.g.* Typical of campaigns before the 1980s.

prerogative powers: constitutional powers resting with the *monarch* but which, in practice, are exercised by the *prime minister*.

- *e.g.* Examples include the power to dissolve *parliament* and call a *general election*, and the power to appoint *cabinet ministers*.

presidential: a style of leadership associated with a president, particularly the president of the USA.

- Both *Margaret Thatcher* and *Tony Blair* have been criticised for adopting a presidential style due to their powerful positions, their aloofness, their dismissive attitudes towards *parliament* and their lack of consultation with *cabinet*. There is some debate, however, over how far comparisons with the USA can be taken as they underestimate the limitations imposed by both the influence of *political parties* in the UK and the power of some *cabinet ministers*.

presidential government: a system of government in which a president is the central figure and *head of government*. See also *parliamentary government*.

- *e.g.* In the USA the president is head of government and is elected independently of the *legislature* (Congress).

president of the European Commission: the head of the *European Commission* is appointed by *member states' heads of government* in the *European Council*, subject to the approval of the *European Parliament*.

- *TIP* Avoid the common mistake of referring to the president of the European Commission as the European president. There is no such position.

press: part of the *media* comprising *broadsheet* and *tabloid* newspapers.

- Broadsheet newspapers (including **The Times**, the **Daily Telegraph** and the **Guardian**) are sometimes referred to as the quality press and contain more detailed political analysis than the tabloids (including the **Sun** and **Daily Mirror**).

- The press in the UK is privately owned and most owners and their newspapers adopt positions that are for or against the *political parties*, their leaders and *policies*. There has been much debate in the UK over the influence of the press, particularly on *voting behaviour*. The *Labour Party* in the 1980s was acutely aware of press bias.

Press Office (Number 10): the part of the *Prime Minister's Office* that looks after the relations with the *media* of the *prime minister* and the government in general.

● In recent years, the Press Office has enjoyed a higher profile and has been accused of becoming involved in deciding on the content of government *policy* rather than merely its presentation. It is run by the prime minister's *press secretary* and is staffed by both permanent *civil servants* and political appointees.

● In 1997, the *Strategic Communications Unit* was added to the Press Office.

press secretary: a government official responsible for looking after relations with the *media*.

● Although all government *departments* have press secretaries, the most prominent is the one in charge of the *prime minister's Press Office*. They are often political appointees rather than career *civil servants* and are also known as *spin doctors*.

▨ **e.g.** Bernard Ingham brought increased influence to the role as *Margaret Thatcher's* press secretary. Alastair Campbell, *Tony Blair's* press secretary between 1997 and 2001, was renowned for his central role in government decision-making.

pressure group: an organisation whose members share common interests and which seeks to influence government usually without putting up *candidates* for election.

● The term 'pressure group' covers a wide range of organisations, including *trade unions*, businesses and charities. Some have millions of members internationally and others have very few. An organisation might temporarily be classified as a pressure group if it becomes affected by a change in government *policy*.

● Interest group is sometimes used synonymously with pressure group, as is *sectional group*.

● Pressure groups are an essential feature of a *pluralist* democratic system.

▨ **TIP** Note the distinctions between *insider* and *outsider groups* and between *cause* or *promotional groups* and sectional groups.

prime minister: the *head of government* who is appointed by the *monarch* by virtue of being leader of the *political party* with the largest representation in the *House of Commons*.

● The prime minister's official title is *first lord of the Treasury*.

● The power of the prime minister continues to be widely debated. Some observers believe that the powers exercised by the prime minister should be subject to more democratic control. Others — whilst recognising the increase in *prime ministerial power* — argue that limitations do exist and that descriptions of *presidential government* or *prime ministerial government* are exaggerations.

prime ministerial government: the theory that the *prime minister* has achieved a dominant and almost *presidential* position to the detriment of traditional *cabinet government*.

● The theory is associated with observations first made in the 1960s by MP R. H. S. Crossman and academic J. P. Mackintosh.

prime ministerial power: *power* exercised by the *prime minister* which has been the subject of academic study involving comparisons between holders of the office.

- Commentators have recognised a general increase in prime ministerial power over time, although some individual office-holders have been judged to have been weaker than their predecessors are. See *prime ministerial government.*

▓ *TIP* Prime ministerial power varies between different prime ministers and during an individual prime minister's tenure of office. This is due to variable factors such as the state of the economy, the size of the parliamentary *majority* and the support of the party enjoyed by a particular prime minister. Variable factors help explain why *Tony Blair* is regarded as being powerful whilst *John Major* was judged to be weak.

prime minister's department: this resource would provide the *prime minister* with *policy* advice and general assistance.

▓ *TIP* Argument surrounds the need for a prime minister's department. On the one hand, the prime minister has an increasing workload whilst not enjoying the resources of the large government *departments* available to most *cabinet* colleagues. On the other hand, the *Prime Minister's Office* has expanded in recent years, and when considered in conjunction with the *Cabinet Office*, there are already considerable resources at a prime minister's disposal. Furthermore, the case for a prime minister being able to match the information and expertise available to *cabinet* colleagues needs to balanced with the democratic desire to avoid enhancing the prime minister's power.

Prime Minister's Office: the resource serving the *prime minister* which comprises four units or offices located at 10 Downing Street.

- The Prime Minister's Office comprises the *Private Office*, the *Press Office*, the *Political Unit* and the *Policy Unit*.

- The office has expanded in recent years to include over 150 staff. It is made up of political appointees, special *advisers* (employed as temporary *civil servants*) and permanent civil servants.

Prime Minister's Question Time: the half-hour in the *House of Commons* every Wednesday when MPs may ask the *prime minister* oral questions.

- The practice was introduced by Prime Minister Harold Macmillan in 1961 and until 1997 there were two quarter-hour sessions each week on a Tuesday and Thursday afternoon.

- Although Question Time provides MPs with an opportunity to scrutinise the prime minister on government policy, the nature of the questions posed and the answers given have both been criticised. In general, MPs from the *opposition parties* seek to embarrass the prime minister, particularly through the use of *supplementary questions* that are not published in advance, whilst MPs from the governing party often ask questions that allow the prime minister to provide a scripted response showing the government in a favourable light. Changes to its format in 1997 halved the number of sessions and extended the length of a single session, but do not appear to have improved the occasion.

- Prime Minister's Question Time is often regarded as merely a short and shallow — but well-publicised — *debate* between the *prime minister* and the *leader of the opposition*.

principal private secretary to the prime minister (PPS): the permanent *civil servant* who runs the *Private Office* in 10 Downing Street.

- Control of access to the *prime minister* means the principal private secretary occupies a central position in government.
- Principal private secretaries are found in all government *departments* advising *cabinet ministers*.
- In 1997, Sir Robin Butler (the *cabinet secretary*) thwarted *Tony Blair*'s attempt to have a political appointee, Jonathan Powell, as principal private secretary. Powell became *chief of staff* instead.

private bill: proposed *legislation* — now relatively rare — which is intended to apply only to a particular company, public body or section of the population. See also *public bill*.

private finance initiative (PFI): see *public–private partnership*.

Private Member's Bill: proposed *legislation* promoted by an MP who is not a government *minister*.

- Due both to a lack of parliamentary time and the difficulty of ensuring voting support, Private Members' Bills usually fail. In fact, less than a quarter of the 741 Private Members' Bills introduced between 1990 and 1997 became law. The chances of success largely depend on government support, not only in terms of votes but also through the allocation of extra time.
- There are three ways in which a Private Member's Bill can be introduced. These are as a *ballot bill*, as a *Ten Minute Rule* bill and through *Standing Order 58*.
- *e.g.* In 1997, Michael Foster introduced a *bill* to ban hunting with dogs that passed its *second reading* but ran out of parliamentary time. In the 1960s, David Steel successfully passed a Private Member's Bill reforming the laws on abortion.

Private Office (No. 10): the part of the *Prime Minister's Office* which manages the *prime minister*'s official engagements, relations with *parliament* and the two-way flow of information with government *departments*.

- The Private Office is run by the prime minister's *principal private secretary* and is staffed mainly by other permanent *civil servants* on secondment from government departments.

privatisation: the transfer of state-owned or nationalised industries to the private sector.

- Although the policy of privatisation is linked with *Margaret Thatcher*, it has continued to be pursued by subsequent governments.
- *e.g.* Shares in British Telecom were sold off to private investors in the 1980s, and in the 1990s British Rail was broken up into separate companies and transferred to the private sector.

Privy Council: originally established as a group of advisers to the *monarch*, it is now composed of senior members of the *government* and *opposition*. See also *Order in Council*.

- Members are appointed by the monarch on the advice of the *prime minister* and are required to swear an oath of secrecy. Membership is for life.
- The Judicial Committee of the Privy Council, the *Law Lords* under another name, acts as the final court of appeal for certain Commonwealth countries.

promotional group: a *pressure group* (also known as a *cause group*) that seeks to promote an interest or idea not of direct personal benefit to its members.

- *e.g.* The Royal Society for the Protection of Birds (RSPB) or the National Society for the Prevention of Cruelty to Children (NSPCC).
- *TIP* Distinguish between promotional (or *cause*) *groups* and *sectional groups*.

proportional electoral system: an *electoral system* featuring *proportional representation*.

- *e.g. Single transferable vote* and *party list*.

proportionality: the effect achieved by *proportional representation* in which the percentage share of the votes won by a *political party* in elections to the *legislature* is reflected in that party's resulting percentage share of the *seats* in that legislature.

proportional representation (PR): a feature of *electoral systems* in which the percentage share of the votes won by a *political party* in elections to the *legislature* is reflected in that party's resulting percentage share of the *seats* in the legislature.

- The system used for elections to the *House of Commons* lacks *proportionality*. In the 2001 *general election,* the *Labour Party* won 42% of the votes, which translated into 63% of the seats, whilst the *Liberal Democrats* won 19% of the votes and 8% of the seats. Many observers argue that PR would be fairer as these percentages would be matched.
- Proportional representation is a central issue in the debate on *electoral reform*, and is favoured by the Liberal Democrats, who feel disadvantaged by the current *first-past-the-post* system. Opponents of PR fear that its likely consequences would be *hung parliaments* and *coalition governments*.
- *e.g. Single transferable vote* and *party list*.
- *TIP* Note that proportional representation is not an electoral system but a feature of certain electoral systems.

prospective model: an explanation of *voting behaviour* which regards a voter's choice of *political party* as being made according to the perceived competence of the parties based on their likely future performance. See also *retrospective model*.

protest vote: a vote cast with the aim of defeating — or at least showing discontent with — a particular *candidate* or *political party*, as opposed to its being a positive expression of support.

- Protest votes are common at the *by-elections*, *European elections* and *local elections*

p

that take place in the middle of a *parliament*. On these occasions, voters might wish to express their discontent by voting against the candidates of the governing party in the knowledge that their votes will not bring about a change of government at *Westminster*.

■ *e.g.* In the 1999 European elections, Labour attracted 26% of the votes and the Conservatives 40%. In view of the *Labour Party*'s lead in *opinion polls* on projected voting at a future *general election*, it is likely that many of the Conservative votes were protest votes (although, of course, there were other factors affecting the results). At the 1997 general election in the Tatton *constituency*, the *independent* candidate Martin Bell benefited from protest votes against the sitting MP Neil Hamilton due to his involvement in the *cash for questions* scandal. Similarly, in the 2001 general election, the independent candidate Richard Taylor was elected as the MP for Wyre Forest after defeating the sitting Labour MP following a campaign against a local hospital closure.

psephology: the study of *elections* and *voting behaviour*.

Public Accounts Committee: the *non-departmental select committee* of the *House of Commons*, established in 1861 to scrutinise the government's accounts and ensure that public money is properly spent.

Public Administration Committee: the *non-departmental select committee* of the *House of Commons* that scrutinises the operations of central government *departments*.

public bill: proposed *legislation* applying to the public as a whole. See also *private bill*.

● Public bills account for the majority of legislation passing through *parliament*.

● The government sponsors most public bills, but around 10% are *Private Members' Bills*.

public opinion: a general sense of the views of the population, expressed at elections and monitored between these times in *opinion polls*.

● Public opinion on specific issues can be gauged using opinion polls or *referendums*. This is more difficult during parliamentary elections when a range of issues and factors influence *voting behaviour*.

public–private partnership: the collaboration between the public and private sectors in the provision of services.

● The *Labour Party*'s supportive attitude towards public–private partnerships is an example of policy resulting from *New Labour*'s ideological position known as the *Third Way*.

■ *e.g.* Labour's private finance initiative (PFI) proposal for the London Underground.

QMV: see *qualified majority voting.*

qualified majority voting (QMV): a weighted system of voting used in the *European Union Council of Ministers.*

- In this system each *member state* is given a weighting according to size of population. Thus, for example, France, Germany and the UK have 10 votes each, Spain has 8, Portugal 5 and Luxembourg 2. The total of weighted votes is 87. For a measure to pass, 62 votes are required, which means that 26 votes (a combination of at least three member states) are needed to block a measure.

- Unanimity amongst member states was originally required to pass most measures in the Council of Ministers but, starting with the *Single European Act* (1986), the number of *policy* areas subject to QMV has been regularly increased (for example, in the treaties of *Maastricht* and *Amsterdam*). The most important decisions, such as those over the accession of new member states, are not subject to QMV.

quango: an unelected body — not run by *civil servants* or *local government* — which is responsible for performing a public service and spending public money.

- It is the acronym for quasi-autonomous non-governmental organisation.

- Both the number of quangos and their responsibilities have expanded rapidly since 1979. This has raised concerns about *power* being exercised by unelected and largely unaccountable officials. The *prime minister*'s power of *patronage* extends to the appointment of many quango heads.

- *e.g.* Depending on the definition used, quangos include the BBC, the Commission for Racial Equality, health service trusts and the regulators of privatised industries such as Ofwat, Oftel and Ofgas.

- *TIP* The description is disputed. According to some people, the word 'non' should be 'national'. Quangos are sometimes referred to as non-departmental public bodies.

quasi-government: a branch of the public sector which is run by unelected government appointees rather than *civil servants* or *local government* officers and which provides a public service and spends public money. See also *quango.*

Queen's Speech: the government's plans for *legislation* in the coming year delivered by the *head of state* in the *House of Lords* at the ceremonial occasion (known as the *State Opening of Parliament*) held at the beginning of a *parliamentary session*.

- The speech is usually given every November.
- Although the words are spoken by the queen, the speech is written by the government.

Questions of Procedure for Ministers: see *Ministerial Code*.

Question Time: the opportunity for MPs or *peers* to ask government *ministers* oral questions in the *House of Commons* or *House of Lords*. See also *Prime Minister's Question Time*.

- Question Time lasts approximately 1 hour each afternoon from Monday to Thursday. Apart from the *prime minister*, who answers questions on a Wednesday amidst greater publicity, government ministers take turns to answer questions on *policy* areas for which they are responsible. Ministers' Question Time, as opposed to Prime Minister's Question Time, is considered a more serious method of *scrutiny*.

quota (for STV): the figure a *candidate* needs to reach to be elected during the counting of votes under the *single transferable vote electoral system*.

- Also known as the Droop quota, the figure varies from election to election and is calculated by dividing the total number of first preference votes cast by the sum of one plus the original number of *seats* to be allocated, adding one to the total.

rational choice model: a *voting behaviour* theory that regards voters as consumers who choose between the *political parties* on the basis of *policies,* past records and the qualities of party leaders.

- The model has gained support since the 1970s and emphasises *instrumental voting* (rational decisions) over *expressive voting* (emotional decisions).
- An important aspect of this model is *issue voting.*

realignment: the development of new long-term attachments between voters and *political parties,* which necessitates a fresh assessment of *voting behaviour* patterns.

- Some argue that increased proportions of the *working class* voting Conservative in the 1980s and of the *middle class* voting Labour since 1997 are evidence for class realignment. Others regard these changes as further evidence for the *class dealignment* of the *electorate* since the 1970s.
- The emergence of a new party — such as the *Social Democratic Party* in 1981 (albeit briefly) — can also cause realignment.

rebellion (in parliament): rare occasion on which MPs defy their *party whips* and vote against their party, also known as a backbench rebellion or revolt.

- Although a breakdown of *party discipline* is regarded as serious in the *House of Commons,* a rebellion rarely leads to a government defeat. The size of a rebellion, in terms of numbers of MPs, is a measure of discontent amongst *backbenchers.*
- *e.g.* In December 1997, a rebellion on the issue of single-parent benefits in the House of Commons saw 47 Labour MPs voting against their party with a further 14 abstentions. However, the measure was still passed. In 1994, the Conservative government's slim *majority* meant it was defeated due to a backbench rebellion on the increase in VAT on domestic fuel.

redress of grievances: a remedy for a *citizen*'s complaint about an administrative action taken by a government body or an organisation funded by public money.

- In the UK, redress of grievances can be sought through a variety of means. These include the court system, *tribunals, ombudsmen* and MPs.

referendum: a vote on a single issue put before the *electorate* by the government, usually in the form of a question requiring a yes or no response.

- Referendums are rare in the UK, although they have been used since the 1970s for issues of constitutional importance. There is much debate on their constitutional position, because they are a feature of *direct democracy* in the UK's system of *representative democracy*.

- **e.g.** To date there has only been one referendum question put before the entire electorate of the UK. This was in 1975 on the issue of continued membership of the *European Economic Community*. The other referendums have concerned *regional government* in Northern Ireland, Scotland and Wales, and whether London should elect a *mayor*. UK-wide referendums have been promised on *electoral reform* and membership of the *single European currency*.

- **TIP** Be able to distinguish between a referendum and an *initiative*.

Referendum Party: a single-issue *political party* that was founded and funded by the late Sir James Goldsmith and which fielded 547 *candidates* in the 1997 *general election*.

- The party advocated a *referendum* on the UK's future in the *European Union*. Although it did not win a *seat* in *parliament*, it had some impact on the election in terms of the issues debated and the results. D. Butler and D. Kavanagh calculate that — together with the *UK Independence Party* — the Referendum Party attracted enough *euro-sceptic* votes to cost the *Conservative Party* three seats.

- The Referendum Party has not fielded candidates in elections since 1997.

regional government: sub-national government proposed by the *Labour Party* as part of its plans for *devolution*.

- Regional government should be distinguished from the smaller geographical areas of *local government*. English regional government, although strictly not devolved, can be found in London, and possible areas for the scheme's future expansion are the northeast and the southwest.

regionalism: the support for regional identities within the UK, particularly in terms of *regional government*.

- Regionalism found favour with the Labour government after 1997, as seen in the establishment of the *Greater London Authority* and plans for regional government in other parts of England.

registered voter: a *citizen* whose name appears on a *constituency*'s *electoral register* and who is thereby entitled to vote in that constituency.

Register of Members' Interests: the record, established in 1975, to combat corruption by detailing payments made to MPs (in bands of £5,000) relating to the provision of services in their capacity as MPs.

- The compilation, maintenance and accessibility of the Register of Members' Interests is supervised by the *parliamentary commissioner for standards*.

- Since the strengthening of the Register of Members' Interests following the *Nolan Report* in 1995, there has been concern that MPs do not declare all their earnings because of the question of what is earned 'in their capacity' as MPs.

- The extension of such *scrutiny* to *peers'* interests became an issue in the 1997–2001 *parliament*.

report stage: the part of the *legislative process*, between the *committee stage* and the *third reading*, when amendments made to a *bill* are considered and further changes may be made.

- The report stage takes place on the floor of the House. There is no report stage if the bill is reported unamended from a *Committee of the Whole House*. This stage is usually combined with the third reading.

representation: the function performed by *representatives* acting or speaking on behalf of another's interests.

- It is performed through *political parties* and *pressure groups*.
- Representation is also a task of MPs in *parliament*. This can occasionally be a source of conflict when an MP is expected to represent the competing interests of party and *constituency*.
- A party's representation in the *House of Commons* is expressed in terms of the numbers of MPs the party has.

representative: someone — often an elected person — who acts or speaks on behalf of another's interests.

- **e.g.** An MP in the *House of Commons*.
- **TIP** The distinction is often drawn between a representative and a *delegate*. The latter receives instructions on how to vote and represent the views of those who have sent him or her, whilst the former is allowed to exercise judgement.

representative democracy: a political system in which *citizens* elect people to make decisions of government on their behalf.

- The UK is a representative democracy with representative institutions such as the *House of Commons*.
- **TIP** Be able to distinguish between representative and *direct democracy*.

representative government: see *representative democracy*.

reselection: the procedure for a *political party* selecting a *candidate* in a *constituency* in which the sitting MP, who represents that party, is not automatically chosen but must submit to a contest.

- Normally, a sitting MP can expect to remain the party's candidate at the next election. In the *Labour Party* between 1980 and 1990, mandatory reselection was adopted to provide for a selection contest and vote amongst members. This worked to the advantage of the *left wing* because it allowed *Constituency Labour Parties* (CLPs) to hold *right-wing* Labour MPs to account with the threat of *deselection*. Changes such as this resulted in the breakaway of some Labour MPs to form the *Social Democratic Party*. A reselection contest now occurs only if one is requested by a majority of *CLP* members, a change symbolic of the re-emergence of the right within the Labour Party.

reshuffle: a *prime minister*'s reallocation of departmental responsibilities between *ministers* within the *cabinet* or the government more widely.

- Reshuffles often happen at the end of the summer to freshen up the government by changing the roles performed by its members. Reshuffles can also be necessitated by a resignation or sacking. A reshuffle may be used by a prime minister to reassert his or her authority.

e.g. In 2001 — following Peter Mandelson's resignation as *secretary of state* for Northern Ireland — John Reid moved from the Scottish Office to this vacated position and Helen Liddell moved from a junior ministerial post to become secretary of state for Scotland.

responsibility: a feature of government implying the *accountability* of government to the people, either directly or through the people's *representatives* in *parliament*. See also *ministerial responsibility, individual responsibility* and *collective responsibility*.

retrospective model: an explanation of *voting behaviour* that regards a voter's choice of *political party* as being made according to the perceived competence of the parties based on their past performance. See also *prospective model*.

returning officer: a local official in each *constituency* who is responsible for the fair operation of electoral procedures, including the nomination of *candidates*, the counting of *ballot papers* and the announcement of the result.

right: see *right-wing*.

rights (civil or human rights): fundamental freedoms possessed by a country's *citizens* — or people in general — that are guaranteed in law, with corresponding obligations imposed on government for their observance.

• Rights in the UK are guaranteed in *common law* in addition to the *European Convention on Human Rights* and the *Human Rights Act*.

e.g. The rights to a fair trial, freedom from torture, freedom from slavery and freedom of expression.

right-wing: ideas and *ideology* associated with capitalism, stressing free enterprise and the *rights* of the individual to be free from government interference.

TIP Political ideology is often portrayed as a spectrum of opinion with *political parties* arranged along it from left to right. Since political parties themselves also contain ranges of opinion, each one has its *left-wing* and right-wing elements.

role responsibility: an aspect of the constitutional *convention* of *individual responsibility*, emphasising a *minister*'s duty to be answerable for the personal performance of duties as a minister, the department's performance and the actions and omissions of subordinates in the *department*.

e.g. Lord Carrington resigned as *foreign secretary* in 1982 following the Argentine invasion of the Falkland Islands.

TIP In 1995, the home secretary Michael Howard sacked Derek Lewis as director of the Prison Service agency. This demonstrated that the creation of *executive agencies* had diluted ministerial *accountability* for failings in government. Some argued that Howard should have resigned, but he claimed that his role responsibility extended only to *policy* and not to operational matters.

Rome, Treaty of (1957): the original treaty establishing the *European Economic Community* (EEC) as a common market or customs union with no customs duties between *member states* and a common external tariff designed to promote the free movement of people, goods, services and capital.

- The six original signatories were Belgium, the Netherlands, Luxembourg, France, Germany and Italy. The UK signed the treaty in 1972.

■ *TIP* There were, in fact, two treaties. As well as that establishing the EEC, there was another establishing Euratom for the coordination of the development of nuclear energy by member states.

royal assent: the final stage of the *legislative process* in which the passage of a *bill* through *parliament* is completed with the *monarch*'s signature.

- This stage of the legislative process is now, by *convention*, automatic. The last occasion on which the monarch refused royal assent was in 1707 when Queen Anne vetoed a Scottish Militia Bill.

- Royal assent is an example of a *prerogative power*.

royal commission: a prestigious independent body established by the government to investigate and report on a matter of national importance and whose recommendations may become government *policy*.

■ *e.g.* The Royal Commission on Reform of the *House of Lords* (also known as the *Wakeham Commission*) was established in 1998 and reported in January 2000.

royal prerogative: see *prerogative powers*.

rule of law: a fundamental feature of the UK *constitution* which includes as its principal elements the equal application of the law to all governments and people, the principle that everyone is innocent until proven guilty, and *judicial independence*.

■ *TIP* A.V. Dicey, writing in the nineteenth century, regarded the rule of law as one of the 'twin pillars of the constitution', the other being *parliamentary sovereignty*.

safe seat: a parliamentary *constituency* which can be relied upon to elect an MP from the same *political party* at every election.

- At *general elections* in which there is an unusually large *swing* against a particular party — such as happened in 1997 — even seats previously regarded as safe may be lost by that party. An example is Michael Portillo's loss of the Conservative seat of Enfield Southgate. At *by-elections*, increased *protest voting* has meant that the loss of a safe seat by an unpopular party in government has become less rare. An example of this occurred in 1994 when a Conservative *majority* of 17,702 was overturned in the Eastleigh by-election.

■ *e.g.* The Conservative seat of Huntingdon and the Labour seat of Sedgefield.

Salisbury Doctrine: the constitutional *convention* that the *House of Lords* does not vote on the *second reading*, and therefore cannot block a *government bill* contained in the election *manifesto*.

- The convention was introduced by Lord Salisbury, Conservative leader in the House of Lords in 1945, and has been extended to include any *bill* appearing in the government's programme for the *session*.

sample: a polling organisation's group of voters selected to represent the *electorate* and consulted to produce *opinion polls*.

- Two methods of sampling are available. Most polls are conducted using a quota sample obtained by finding respondents who together match the age, sex, class and other characteristics of the electorate. The other method uses a probability sample in which every nth name is chosen from the *electoral register*.

Scottish Executive: the devolved *cabinet* (with *executive* powers) comprising *Members of the Scottish Parliament* and presided over by the *first minister* for Scotland. See *devolution*.

Scottish National Party (SNP): the left-of-centre *nationalist* party, represented by MPs in the *Westminster Parliament* and *Members of the Scottish Parliament*, which supported *devolution* as a step towards its ultimate goal of an independent Scotland within the *European Union*.

Scottish Parliament: the devolved *legislature*, created in 1999 after the Scottish *electorate* gave its approval for *devolution* in a *referendum* in 1997.

- It is based in Edinburgh and comprises 129 elected *Members of the Scottish Parliament.*
- The Scottish Parliament has more legislative powers than the devolved assemblies in Wales and Northern Ireland, including the ability to pass primary *legislation* (which means enabling legislation is not required from the *Westminster Parliament* granting it authority to pass secondary legislation) and to vary the rate of income tax by plus or minus 3%.

scrutiny: supervision of government institutions, including their elected and unelected officials, to ensure that they are operating as they should.
- A function of *parliament* is to scrutinise government *ministers* and *departments,* and to hold them to account. MPs are also scrutinised by committees in the *House of Commons* such as the *Standards and Privileges Committee.*
- The *media* also have a role in scrutinising government.

SDLP: see *Social Democratic and Labour Party.*

SDP: see *Social Democratic Party.*

seat: an elected position in a *legislature* that is often an alternative description for a parliamentary *constituency.*
- The size of a *political party*'s *majority* or *representation* in the *House of Commons* is often expressed in terms of seats.

second chamber: a subordinate body in a *bicameral legislature,* such as the UK *House of Lords.* See also *Wakeham Commission, Wakeham Report* and *unicameral legislature.*
- There has been much debate surrounding the future role and composition of the *Westminster Parliament*'s second chamber.

second reading: a *debate* and subsequent vote on the main principles of a *bill* during its passage through the *House of Commons* and *House of Lords.*
- The second reading of a *bill* forms part of the *legislative process* between the *first reading* and the *committee stage.*
- This stage usually takes place on the floor of each chamber in *parliament,* although non-controversial bills may have their second reading in a committee.

secretary of state: the official title of a *cabinet minister* who heads a government *department* or *ministry.*
- *e.g.* The secretary of state for health.

sectional group: a *pressure group* which seeks to represent the shared interests of a particular section of society.
- Members of a sectional group usually derive personal benefit, often seen in economic terms, from the activities of the group.
- *e.g.* The Law Society or the National Union of Teachers.
- *TIP* Distinguish between sectional groups and *promotional* (or *cause*) groups.

select committee: a parliamentary committee with the function of investigating and scrutinising both the *executive* (through examining public *policy* and administration) and aspects of the workings of the *legislature.*

- Select committees in the *House of Commons* and *House of Lords* take oral and written evidence and publish reports.
- There are currently 16 departmental select committees, each examining a government *department* (e.g. the Culture, Media and Sport Committee chaired by the Labour MP Gerald Kaufman). Each departmental select committee has 11 MPs as members.
- *Non-departmental select committees* can be permanent (e.g. the *Public Accounts Committee*) or ad hoc (e.g. the *Committee on Standards in Public Life*).
- **TIP** The distinction should be drawn between *departmental select committees* (which are only in the House of Commons) and non-departmental select committees. Take care to distinguish between select committees and *standing committees*.

Select Committee on European Legislation: the *non-departmental select committee* of the *House of Commons* which considers *European Union legislation* proposed by the *European Commission* or the *Council of Ministers*, and which can refer proposals requiring further *scrutiny* to a *standing committee*.

- Concern has been expressed that this committee lacks both the powers and resources to carry out its function.

Select Committee on Standards and Privileges: a new *non-departmental select committee* established in the wake of the *cash for questions* scandal to oversee the conduct and interests of MPs.

- The *parliamentary commissioner for standards* supervises the *Register of Members' Interests* and reports to the Select Committee on Standards and Privileges.

separation of powers: a feature of democratic government in which three distinct branches of government — the *executive*, the *legislature* and the *judiciary* — operate independently of each other.

- The lack of a separation of powers in the UK is evident from the convention that members of the *cabinet* (part of the executive) must be members of either the *House of Commons* or the *House of Lords* (the legislature). Indeed, the *Lord Chancellor* occupies a position in all three branches of government. This is known as a *fusion of powers*.
- **e.g.** A separation of powers is clearly identifiable in the federal government of the USA.

Service First: a Labour initiative in 1998 to replace the *Citizen's Charter* and to give the general public certain guarantees relating to the provision of public services.

- As was the case with the Citizen's Charter, a *Cabinet Office* team runs the programme.

session (parliamentary): the division of time in the life of a *parliament* beginning with the annual *state opening*, and finishing usually less than a year later with a break in proceedings officially known as a prorogation.

shadow cabinet: a *House of Commons* team from the main *opposition* party whose function is to mirror the *ministers* in the *cabinet* and scrutinise their performance.

- The shadow cabinet plays an important role in holding the government to account, most visibly in the *media* and when asking questions of their government counterparts at *Question Time*. The shadow cabinet is, in effect, the cabinet-in-waiting, thus presenting a choice to the *electorate* at a *general election*.
- When the *Labour Party* is in opposition, the *Parliamentary Labour Party* elects the shadow cabinet.
- **e.g.** There is a shadow *chancellor of the exchequer* and a shadow *home secretary*.

shortlist: the choice of possible *parliamentary candidates* presented to members of a *constituency* party as part of the selection process.

- This is a common feature of the three main parties' candidate selection processes. However, rules on how shortlists are compiled and who may appear on them differ between the parties. An attempt by the *Labour Party* to increase female representation by insisting on *women-only shortlists* was declared illegal in the courts as it was deemed to discriminate against men.

short-term factors: transitory influences affecting *voting behaviour* which, because they often change from one election to the next, contribute to *volatility* in the *electorate* and less predictable results. See also *long-term factors*.

- Short-term factors such as how the party leaders are perceived, the state of the economy, the attitudes adopted by newspapers and the *feelgood factor* are considered to have become more important amongst the influences affecting voting behaviour since the 1970s.

simple majority (or simple plurality): the difference in the number of votes between the winning *candidate* or *political party* and the candidate or party in second place.

- This difference describes the extent of the victory resulting from an election.
- The winner's *majority* in an individual *constituency* is expressed in terms of the simple majority, rather than the *overall majority*. For example, the South West Surrey constituency in the 2001 *general election* saw the Conservative candidate, Virginia Bottomley, winning with a majority of 861. However, this difference, between her 22,462 votes and the 21,601 won by the Liberal Democrat candidate, ignored the 5,529 votes won by the other candidates.

simple plurality: see *simple majority*.

- **TIP** The *electoral system* used for elections to the *Westminster Parliament* is commonly known as *first-past-the-post* but is more correctly called simple plurality in *single-member constituencies*.

single currency: see *single European currency*.

Single European Act (1986): the amendment to the *Treaty of Rome* to establish a single internal market between *member states* of the *European Economic Community* (now the *European Union*) and which gave more power to the *European Parliament* and extended the use of *qualified majority voting* in the *Council of Ministers*.

- At the time, *Prime Minister Margaret Thatcher* supported the Single European Act in the interests of free market economics, deregulation and economic growth.
- Jacques Delors, the then *president of the European Commission*, supported the Single European Act in the interests of promoting further European *integration*.

single European currency (euro): a currency created with *European Monetary Union*, and advanced by the *Maastricht Treaty*.

- The euro's notes and coins will replace the national currencies of most *European Union member states* in 2002.
- The adoption of the single European currency is regarded as the most significant step towards both economic and political integration in the EU. Although most adopted the currency to be phased in from 1 January 1999, the UK was one of three member states not to join *Euroland*.
- All major UK *political parties* promise a *referendum* before a decision is taken on whether to adopt the euro, although there is disagreement on when this should be held. In the 2001 *general election*, the euro was a *Conservative Party* issue in a campaign where its hostility to the euro was particularly marked in contrast to the support of the other two main parties.

single-member constituency: a geographical area represented by one elected official.

- Single-member constituencies may be contrasted with the *multi-member constituencies* used in more *proportional electoral systems* (such as the *single transferable vote* used in *European elections* in Northern Ireland and the *hybrid electoral systems* used for elections to the *Scottish Parliament* and the *Welsh Assembly*).
- *e.g.* The *constituency* of Taunton is represented by one MP at the *Westminster Parliament*, as are all the other constituencies.

single-party system: a political system in which only one *political party* is allowed by law to contest elections and form the government.

- *e.g.* Under the Communist Party, the former USSR was a single-party system. Such systems are usually undemocratic and authoritarian.

single transferable vote (STV): an *electoral system* featuring *proportional representation* in which voters are required to rank *candidates* in order of preference, and which employs *multi-member constituencies*.

- Candidates are elected by reaching a *quota* (also known as the Droop quota). This figure, which varies from election to election, is calculated by dividing the total number of first preference votes cast by the sum of the one plus the original number of *seats* to be allocated, adding one to the total. The first preference votes are counted first, then the second and so on, until the quota has been reached by the number of members to be elected in that constituency.
- STV is the electoral system advocated by the *Liberal Democrats* for use in elections to the *Westminster Parliament*.
- *e.g.* This system is used for elections to the Republic of Ireland *legislature* and for *European elections* in Northern Ireland.

S

Sinn Fein: the Northern Irish, Catholic, republican *political party* which supports the *Good Friday Agreement*.

● Sinn Fein is also known as the political wing of the *Irish Republican Army* (IRA).

sleaze: the term coined by the *media* — associated mainly with Conservative MPs in the years preceding the 1997 *general election* — to describe behaviour that brings a political party, and often the *House of Commons*, into disrepute.

● Before the 1997 general election, the term sleaze covered a range of activities, usually involving hypocrisy and, occasionally, illegality, including extra-marital affairs (for example, Rod Richards MP) and alleged corruption, such as the *cash for questions* affair (Neil Hamilton MP).

● The *Committee on Standards in Public Life* (*Nolan Committee*) was established as a result of the sleaze associated with the cash for questions affair.

Smith, John (1938–1994): the former Labour MP for Monklands East and leader of the *Labour Party* from 1992 until his sudden death following a heart attack in 1994.

● Smith is credited with continuing the modernisation of the Labour Party begun by his predecessor *Neil Kinnock*. Significantly, he secured the adoption of *one member, one vote* in 1993.

Smith Square: the location in London of Conservative Party *Central Office*.

SNP: see *Scottish National Party*.

social class: a category of people sharing common characteristics, reflecting divisions in society, usually determined by economic factors such as income, inherited wealth and occupation, but also relating to family background and lifestyle.

● Definitions of social class vary, but an economic relationship is usually a central feature. In the nineteenth century, Karl Marx identified two classes: capitalists earned their living through investments in land and businesses; the *working class* sold their labour to capitalists in exchange for wages.

● The classes most commonly identified in the UK are the *middle class* and the working class.

● A more detailed and widely used definition of social class is that developed by the Institute of Practitioners in Advertising. This classification established six divisions:

Class A: higher managerial, administrative or professional
Class B: intermediate managerial, administrative or professional
Class C1: junior managerial, administrative or professional, and supervisory or clerical
Class C2: skilled manual
Class D: semi-skilled and unskilled manual
Class E: state pensioners with no other earnings, casual workers and the long-term unemployed

■ *TIP* Social class is an important factor in determining political allegiances and the way people vote. See *class alignment* and *class voting*.

social democracy: the political *ideology* that accepts the existence and continuation of a capitalist society, but which is interested in achieving a more equitable distribution of wealth within that society.

▨ *TIP* Rather than *socialism*, many observers regard the term 'social democracy' as a more accurate description of *Labour Party*'s ideology.

Social Democratic and Labour Party (SDLP): the Northern Irish, Catholic, *nationalist* party which supports the *Good Friday Agreement*.

Social Democratic Party (SDP): a *political party* founded in 1981 by prominent *right-wing* members of the *Labour Party* unhappy with what they regarded as its increasing dominance by the *left wing*.

- The SDP's founding members — the Gang of Four — were Roy Jenkins, David Owen, Bill Rodgers and Shirley Williams.
- Initially, the party enjoyed popularity and, in alliance with the *Liberal Party*, secured 26% of the votes in the 1983 *general election* and 22% in 1987. Following the 1987 general election, most members of the party merged with the Liberals to form the *Liberal Democratic Party*. The rump SDP lasted until 1990.

Social Exclusion Unit: established in 1998 as part of the *Cabinet Office* with the aim of improving *policy* delivery in areas such as drugs, unemployment and poverty that involve more than one government *department*.

- The Social Exclusion Unit and the *Performance and Innovation Unit* are key elements in providing what the Labour government calls 'joined-up government' (i.e. the coordination of government departments).

socialism: a political *ideology* that provides a critique of capitalism and advocates fundamental changes to the structure of society to improve the welfare of the majority *working class*, particularly through the redistribution of wealth. See also *social democracy*.

- Socialist ideology is traditionally associated with the *Labour Party*, although this association has been weakened with the advent of *New Labour*.

Socialist Alliance: *left-wing* coalition, for electoral purposes, between Militant and the *Socialist Workers' Party* which fielded about 170 *candidates* in the 2001 *general election*.

Socialist Labour Party: a *political party* founded in 1996 by the miners' leader Arthur Scargill as a *left-wing* breakaway from the *Labour Party*.

- The establishment of the Socialist Labour Party was prompted by the Labour Party's adoption of a new *Clause IV*, which Scargill regarded as evidence of an abandonment of the principles of *socialism*. It attracts limited support and in the 2001 *general election* Arthur Scargill polled only 912 votes in the Hartlepool *constituency* and lost his *deposit*.

Socialist Workers' Party: an extreme *left-wing minor party* founded by Tony Cliff, a former *Labour Party* member expelled for being a Trotskyite.

soundbite: a pithy political remark or slogan that is designed to be a memorable summary of an aspect of *ideology* or *policy*, lending itself to reporting in the *media*.

■ *e.g.* The *Labour Party*'s 'tough on crime, tough on the causes of crime' before the 1997 *general election* and the *Conservative Party*'s 'in Europe, not run by Europe' before the 2001 general election.

sovereignty: the power, usually ascribed to a country, to make decisions of government without the influence of external forces. See also *parliamentary sovereignty*.

● The extent of the UK's sovereignty is the subject of much debate. Economic sovereignty has been limited by global economic interdependence, and *euro-sceptics* are concerned about the ways in which European *integration* and the development of the institutions of the *European Union* have undermined national political sovereignty.

speaker: the presiding officer in the *House of Commons*, whom MPs elect to chair *debates* by calling MPs to speak and ensure that procedural rules are followed.

● The speaker is a politically impartial figure who, although elected to the House of Commons to represent a *constituency* as a member of a *political party*, must renounce party political allegiances. By tradition, the speaker does not run for re-election in his or her constituency under a party label and the major parties do not field candidates in the speaker's constituency. The speaker does not participate in debates and only votes in the event of a tie. The speaker appoints the chairpersons of *standing committees*.

● The speaker is assisted by a number of deputy speakers who take turns to chair *debates*.

● The speaker preserves order in the House of Commons through the threat or imposition of a number of sanctions. MPs can be asked to withdraw remarks that use 'unparliamentary language', they can be suspended, and the speaker can suspend proceedings in the rare event of general disorder.

■ *e.g.* The current speaker is Michael Martin. Following the retirement of Betty Boothroyd, he was elected in 2000.

■ *TIP* Contrast the neutrality of the House of Commons speaker with the party political position of the speaker in the US House of Representatives. The latter achieves his or her position by being the leading figure in the *majority* party.

special adviser: see *adviser*.

special standing committee: a *standing committee* that calls witnesses and considers a *bill* in general before the bill is scrutinised clause by clause.

● Special standing committees are not the norm, although those who criticise the limited remit of ordinary standing committees have advocated their more frequent use.

■ *e.g.* In the 1997–2001 *parliament*, a special standing committee examined the Asylum Bill.

spin: news management by *political parties* intended to ensure favourable reporting in the *media*.

● All political parties attempt to influence the way news items are reported: for instance, through the use of press releases. *New Labour* has been accused of having an obsession with spin rather than with the substance of its *policies*.

spin doctor: a term often used pejoratively, to describe someone working for a *politician* whose role is to manage the way items appear in the news and ensure that reporting favourable to their employer appears through the *media*.

- A spin doctor may be employed full-time as a press officer or on a consultancy basis. The work of spin doctors is particularly evident during election *campaigns*. Labour's use of spin doctors after 1997 attracted criticism on the grounds that they were political appointees working for the benefit of the *Labour Party*, rather than as neutral and *non-partisan* government employees. Charlie Whelan — who was employed by Gordon Brown in the *Treasury* — was accused of briefing journalists against Brown's political rivals in the government.

e.g. The prime example is Alastair Campbell, *Prime Minister Tony Blair*'s chief *press secretary* from 1997 to 2001.

spoilt ballot: a *ballot paper* that does not count for a *candidate* because the vote has not been recorded in the correct manner and the intention of the voter is therefore deemed to be unclear.

- Some spoilt ballots may be an indication of protest against the choice of candidates or the way the election has been conducted.

Standards and Privileges Committee: see *Select Committee on Standards and Privileges*.

standing committee: a parliamentary committee, comprising 18–25 members of the *House of Commons* or *House of Lords*, whose function is to scrutinise the details of proposed *legislation* as part of the *legislative process*.

- A *bill* is considered by a standing committee during the *committee stage* of its passage through *parliament*.
- Despite their name, standing committees are not permanent, but are established for consideration of a particular bill and then disbanded. Letters of the alphabet distinguish standing committees and Standing Committee C usually considers *Private Members' Bills*.
- The membership of standing committees in the House of Commons is decided by consultation between the senior MPs' *Committee of Selection* and *party whips*. The relevant government *minister* and spokesmen from *opposition* parties are always members of the committee, together with others who have an expertise or particular interest in the bill. The party composition of standing committees reflects that in the main chamber. Through the operation of *party discipline,* the government can thus ensure passage of its legislation through this stage and may make minor *amendments*. The government can also employ the *guillotine* to cut short *debate* and guarantee the passage of its bills.

TIP Take care to distinguish between standing committees and *select committees*.

Standing Order 58: the procedural *House of Commons* rule allowing a *backbench MP* to introduce a *bill* without *debate* if a day's notice is given to the *speaker*.

- Standing Order 58 is one of three ways of introducing a *Private Member's Bill*. Most bills introduced in this way do not complete their passage into *legislation*.

S

standing orders: the rules governing the procedures of the *House of Commons*.

state: organisation, usually referring to a country, that exercises, through its institutions, governmental *power* over its *citizens*.

State Opening of Parliament: the ceremonial occasion — held annually and usually in November — at which the *monarch* formally begins a new *parliamentary session*. See also *Queen's Speech*.

statute: law created as the result of a *bill* completing its passage through *parliament*.

- Also known as an *act of parliament*, it achieves its status as a law by being voted through the *House of Commons* and the *House of Lords* and receiving *royal assent*.
- *Parliamentary sovereignty* means that statute law is the highest form of law in the UK.

Stormont: see *Northern Ireland Assembly*.

Strategic Communications Unit: the team of *civil servants* and special *advisers* whose function is to coordinate the government's relations with the *media*.

- The Strategic Communications Unit was established by the Labour government in 1997 and is attached to the *Press Office* in the *Prime Minister's Office*.

STV: see *single transferable vote*.

subsidiarity: the *European Union* principle that decisions should be taken at the lowest level of government (local, regional, national or international) compatible with efficiency and practicality.

- The principle implies power being exercised nearest to those most closely affected and the avoidance of over-centralisation.
- ▧ *TIP* An interesting comparison may be drawn between subsidiarity in the EU and the 10th Amendment to the US Constitution. The amendment was introduced to guarantee the rights of state governments and ordinary citizens and is often invoked by those attempting to prevent the further expansion of the powers of the federal government in Washington DC.

supplementary (supplementary question): an oral question that an MP is allowed in addition to that which he or she has tabled for *Question Time*.

- Each MP who has tabled a question is allowed one supplementary. Because the content of supplementary questions is not known in advance by the *minister*, this opportunity is often used to catch the minister out and score political points.

supplementary vote system: an *electoral system* that elects *candidates* in *single-member constituencies* and which requires voters to make a first and second preference choice of candidates on the *ballot paper*.

- If a candidate attracts more than 50% of the first preference votes cast, then he or she is elected. If no candidate wins more than 50% of these votes, then the two candidates with the most first preference votes remain in contention and all other candidates are eliminated. The second preference votes from the ballot papers initially allocated to these eliminated candidates are then taken into account. Of the remaining two candidates, the one with more first and second preference votes combined is elected.

supranationalism: the cooperation between governments and their appointees at a level that ignores national interests and considerations, as featured in the *European Commission* and the *European Court of Justice*.

swing: the calculation on a national or *constituency* basis of the proportion of voters changing from one *political party* to another between elections.

- The swing is calculated by adding the rise in one party's share of the vote to the fall in the other party's share and then dividing the sum by two.
- The swing from the Conservatives to Labour in the 1997 *general election* of more than 10% was the largest in any general election since 1945.
- The swings in the 1997 and 2001 general elections were not uniform across the country. Variations of swing from one constituency to the next are evidence of increased levels of *tactical voting*.

tabloid: a newspaper printed on A3-size paper and associated with more popular journalism. See also *broadsheet*.

■ *e.g.* The *Sun*, the *Daily Mirror*, the *Daily Mail*.

tactical voting: the electoral behaviour of a voter who ignores his or her favourite *candidate* and votes instead for the candidate most likely to defeat that voter's least favoured candidate.

● There was considerable evidence for tactical voting at the 1997 *general election* amongst voters seeking to secure the *Conservative Party*'s removal from government. Tactical voting results in fewer *wasted votes* and helps explain how the *Liberal Democrats* increased the number of *seats* won from 1992 to 1997 on a reduced share of the vote.

● During the 2001 general election, an independent website (www.tacticalvoter.net) advised voters on tactical voting. In southwest Surrey, for example, Labour voters were encouraged to vote Liberal Democrat as the best hope of defeating the Conservative candidate.

■ *e.g.* In 1997, a significant number of Liberal Democrat supporters voted Labour in Rugby and Kenilworth and replaced the sitting Conservative member. Similarly, the Liberal Democrats in Taunton won a Conservative-held seat when Labour supporters switched their vote.

target seat: a *constituency* where a *political party* feels it has a realistic chance of gaining the seat from another party and towards which, consequently, it devotes more resources.

● Attention to particular target seats is a feature of *post-modern campaigning*.

■ *e.g.* In the 1997 *general election*, the *Labour Party* targeted the Worcester constituency. In 2001, the *Liberal Democrats'* target seats included Totnes.

taskforce: a team of *civil servants* established to offer *policy* advice on a particular issue.

● Since the Labour government came to power in 1997, the creation of taskforces has become a popular device to advise on issues not fitting neatly within the responsibility of a single government *department*.

■ *e.g.* The Better Regulation Taskforce.

Ten Minute Rule: procedural rule of the *House of Commons* which allows a *backbench MP* 10 minutes to present the case for a new *bill*.

- The Ten Minute Rule is one of three ways of introducing a *Private Member's Bill*. Whilst it is extremely rare for such *bills* to complete their passage into *legislation*, the rule is popular amongst MPs as a way of gaining publicity for an issue.

Thatcher, Margaret (1925–): the former Conservative MP for Finchley, leader of the *Conservative Party* from 1975 to 1990, and *prime minister* from 1979 to 1990.

- Thatcher is the only woman to have been prime minister and was the longest-serving prime minister of the twentieth century. She was renowned as a strong and uncompromising leader.
- Her period in office saw considerable changes in British society, as a result of a legislative programme following an *ideology* that came to be described as *Thatcherism*. She supported the operation of free market economics, privatised state-owned industries and introduced *legislation* restricting *trade union* activity. She was prime minister during the Falklands War.
- Thatcher's popularity declined after her third *general election* victory in 1987, and she resigned as party leader and prime minister in 1990 following a leadership challenge from Michael Heseltine. Since her resignation, Thatcher has continued to voice the *euro-sceptic* opinions that had become increasingly evident whilst she was still in office.

Thatcherism: the dominant *Conservative Party ideology* since the 1970s, associated with the leadership of *Margaret Thatcher*. See also *neo-liberalism* and *New Right*.

- Central to Thatcherism is the support of free market economics. The ideology promotes free enterprise, reform of the public sector and *privatisation*, and it regards *trade union* activity as an obstacle to economic growth. The intellectual roots of Thatcherism can be traced to Sir Keith Joseph, a *cabinet minister* under Thatcher, and to *think-tanks* such as the *Adam Smith Institute*, the *Centre for Policy Studies* and the *Institute of Economic Affairs*.

think-tank: a *pressure group* which conducts research and formulates *policy* ideas with the aim of influencing government decision-makers through the strength of its intellectual argument.

- Think-tanks usually have recognisable *ideologies*. Different think-tanks have been influential in policy formulation in recent governments, particularly those of *Tony Blair* and *Margaret Thatcher*.
- *e.g.* The *Adam Smith Institute* and the *Institute for Public Policy Research*.

third party: the *political party* best placed to provide an electoral challenge to the traditionally dominant *Conservatives* and *Labour Parties*.

- The third party has changed over time and can differ from region to region. The main third party across the UK is the *Liberal Democrats*, though in Scotland and Wales the *Scottish National Party* and *Plaid Cymru* are considered third parties.

third reading: the part of the *legislative process* immediately after the *report stage* involving a *debate* and vote on the whole *bill*.

- The third reading takes place on the floor of the House and is usually combined with the report stage.

Third Way: the *ideology* associated with *New Labour* and *Tony Blair*.

- Third Way advocates claim its attraction exists in its position being neither traditionally *left wing* nor *right wing*. The Third Way emphasises both self-help and a role for the *state*.
- Critics of the Third Way claim that it is a non-ideology with no intellectual consistency and that it is merely a slogan or *soundbite*.

three-line whip: the instruction from the *party whips* to MPs indicating that attendance is essential at the *House of Commons* for a particular vote. See also *withdrawal of the whip*.

- Disciplinary measures by the whips are likely to result if an MP ignores or defies a three-line whip.
- The size of Labour's *majority* since 1997 has meant that MPs can take advantage of *pairing* arrangements on votes subject to three-line whips.
- Weekly instructions are issued to a party's MPs from the whips' office. Less important votes are accompanied by *one* and *two-line whips*.

Tory Party: the *political party* that gave rise to the *Conservative Party* in the nineteenth century. The term Tory is now used interchangeably with Conservative. See *one-nation conservatism*.

- *TIP* Tories are occasionally referred to as a faction of the Conservative Party.

Trades Union Congress (TUC): an umbrella group or *peak association* that represents many *trade unions* and therefore both seeks and is sought by the government for consultation.

- The TUC enjoys formal links with the *Labour Party*.

trade union: an organisation that represents a group of workers in negotiations with its employers and, as a *pressure group*, seeks to influence the government in its employment, trade and industrial *policies*. See also *block vote* and *one member, one vote*.

- Trade unions helped found the *Labour Party* in the nineteenth century. Many trade unions are *affiliated* to the Labour Party and play a part in its internal procedures.
- Trade unions can be categorised as *sectional groups* and — particularly during periods of Labour government — can achieve *insider group* status.

- *e.g.* The National Union of Mineworkers (NUM) and Unison.

Treasury: a part of the *civil service* headed by the *chancellor of the exchequer*, and responsible for managing the UK economy by setting levels of taxation and allocating funds between government *departments*.

- The Treasury is traditionally regarded as the most important government department. This is illustrated by the fact that it has two *cabinet ministers*, the chancellor of the exchequer and the chief secretary to the Treasury.

Treaty on European Union: see *Maastricht Treaty*.

tribunal: a body of people whose function is to arbitrate between *citizens* and officials of a government *department* or *executive agency* against which they have a complaint.

- Tribunals are one of the means through which a citizen can seek *redress of grievances*.
- *e.g.* Supplementary Benefits Appeal Tribunal.

tripartism: a style of decision-making evident after the Second World War, which involved consultation between the government, employers and *trade unions*.

- Tripartism fell out of favour during *Margaret Thatcher*'s period in office.
- Also known as *corporatism*, British tripartism is associated with the *National Economic Development Council*, which was established in 1961 and abolished by *John Major* in 1992.

TUC: see *Trades Union Congress*.

turnout: a measure of the level of voter participation in elections expressed as the percentage of *registered voters* who actually voted.

- The low and falling level of turnout in UK elections is considered to indicate apathy amongst the *electorate*. At the 2001 *general election*, the 59% turnout was the lowest since 1918. In 1997, turnout was 71%, the lowest since 1935. *Opinion polls* at the 2001 general election indicated that 77% of those who did not vote believed their votes did not matter, and 53% said an influencing factor was that the result was a foregone conclusion.
- Turnout at *local elections* and *European elections* is traditionally even lower than at general elections, and in the 1999 European elections the figure was below 25%. Turnout is higher in elections in other European countries, although in recent US presidential elections the turnout has been about 50%.

two-line whip: an instruction to MPs from the *party whips* indicating compulsory *House of Commons* attendance for a particular vote, unless the MP has arranged to be absent under the *pairing* system.

- Weekly instructions are issued to a party's MPs from the whips' office. More important votes are accompanied by a *three-line whip* and less important votes by a *one-line whip*.

two-party system: a political system in which two *political parties* compete in elections and, usually, alternate in government, with other parties enjoying little electoral success and political *power*.

- *e.g.* The *party system* involving the Democrats and Republicans in the USA.
- *TIP* Because of the success of *third parties* and also *minor parties* since the 1970s, there is some debate as to whether the UK is best described as a two-party system.

UFF: see *Ulster Freedom Fighters.*

UK Independence Party (UKIP): a *political party* founded in 1993 to advocate the UK's withdrawal from the *European Union.*

- Although the UKIP normally performs poorly in elections, it achieved its most notable success with the election of three *Members of the European Parliament* in the 1999 *European elections.* In the 2001 *general election,* it fielded *candidates* in most *constituencies* and campaigned on the issue of retaining the pound and not joining the *single European currency.* None of its candidates was elected and it was considered to have made little, if any, impact on the results.

UKIP: see *UK Independence Party.*

Ulster Freedom Fighters (UFF): a Northern Irish, Protestant and *loyalist* paramilitary organisation.

Ulster Unionist Party (UUP): a Northern Irish, Protestant and *unionist political party* that supports the *Good Friday Agreement.*

Ulster Volunteer Force (UVF): a Northern Irish, Protestant and *loyalist* paramilitary organisation.

ultra vires: Latin expression meaning 'beyond the powers'.

- During the exercise of *judicial review* a court is called upon to rule on whether a government official has acted ultra vires: that is, without the authorisation of the law.

uncodified constitution: arrangements for government that are not contained in a single, legally *entrenched* document. See also *codified constitution, written constitution* and *unwritten constitution.*

- An uncodified constitution details the composition and responsibilities of government institutions and describes government institutions' relations both with each other and with the country's *citizens.*

- *e.g.* The UK *constitution* is found in a variety of sources, in contrast to that of the USA, which has a codified constitution written in 1787. Whether a codified or *uncodified* constitution is better is the subject of debate involving issues of flexibility, reliability and certainty.

■ *TIP* The constitution of the UK is better described as uncodified, rather than unwritten, as many of its sources are indeed written.

under-representation: a disproportionate number in a representative body that reflects poorly the composition of the *electorate*.

● With 115 women MPs elected in the 2001 *general election* — a slight decrease since 1997 — the female population is under-represented in the *House of Commons*. Women are under-represented in the *cabinet* too, despite an increase in their number to seven.

● Black people and Asians, those with a *working-class* background and those who received a state school education are also under-represented in the House of Commons.

● The term 'under-representation' also describes the effect of the *electoral system* in returning a small number of Liberal Democrat MPs when compared to the number of votes cast for the party in general elections. Similarly, those who vote for the *Conservative Party* in Scotland and Wales are under-represented in the House of Commons.

unicameral legislature: a legislative body comprising one chamber or house. See also *bicameral legislature*.

■ *e.g.* The *Scottish Parliament*, the *European Parliament* and the Israeli Knesset are unicameral legislatures.

unionist: either a member of a *trade union* or a supporter of Northern Ireland remaining as part of the UK.

■ *e.g.* The main unionist *political parties* in Northern Ireland are the *Ulster Unionist Party* and the *Democratic Unionist Party*.

unitary authority: a type of *local government* with all services provided by a single body rather than through a two-tier structure of *district councils* and a *county council*.

■ *e.g.* The Isle of Wight.

unitary state: a system in which the central authority holds governmental *power* exclusively with no autonomous powers residing in any other body. See also *federalism*.

■ *e.g.* The UK is a unitary state. Although there are levels of government other than the national government in London, the *Westminster Parliament* can restrict their powers and even abolish them. Constitutionally, this remains the case even since *devolution*, despite whatever practical obstacles there might be to limiting the powers of the *Scottish Parliament* and the *Welsh Assembly*.

unwritten constitution: arrangements for government, detailing the composition and responsibilities of the institutions of government and describing their relations both with each other and with the country's *citizens*, which are not written down. See also *written constitution, codified constitution* and *uncodified constitution*.

■ *TIP* The UK is frequently (and confusingly) described as having an unwritten constitution. This is not the case. The UK has an *uncodified constitution* that is partially written (in certain *acts of parliament*, for instance) and partially unwritten (in constitutional *conventions*).

usual channels: a parliamentary expression to describe how the business of the *House of Commons* and the *House of Lords* is arranged between the two main *political parties*.

- *Debates* and committee business are described as being arranged through the usual channels when organised by the *party whips* and the *leader of the House* and the shadow leader of the House.

U-turn: a significant, and usually sudden, change of *policy* by a *political party*.

- *e.g.* In 1999, the new shadow chancellor of the exchequer, Michael Portillo, announced policy U-turns by the *Conservative Party* on support for the minimum wage and the independence of the Bank of England to set the level of interest rates.

UUP: see *Ulster Unionist Party*.

UVF: see *Ulster Volunteer Force*.

veto: the right to block a decision even against the wishes of all others involved in the decision-making process.

- **e.g.** Although most *European Union Council of Ministers* decisions are taken by a *qualified majority vote*, a *member state* is still able to exercise a veto over some important decisions, such as applications from potential member states to join the EU.

volatility: a measure of how voters change in their support for *political parties* from one election to the next.

- Since the relative stability of *voting behaviour* in the 1950s, electoral volatility, linked to *class dealignment* and *partisan dealignment*, has increased.
- **TIP** It is important to distinguish between overall and net electoral volatility. The former describes the total amount of vote-switching in the *electorate*, whereas the latter (measured on the Pedersen Index) refers to how much the parties' shares of the vote have changed between elections. It is therefore possible for overall volatility to be high and net volatility to be low. This was observed to be the case between 1979 and 1992 when the *Conservative Party*'s share of the vote fell by a relatively small figure, from 43.9% to 41.9%, indicating a low net volatility. At the same time, however, high levels of overall volatility could be seen in the considerable degree of switching amongst voters both towards and away from the party.

vote: an expression of a preference, usually involving a choice between *candidates* in an *election*, but also in a *referendum* and during proceedings in a *legislature*.

- The term is also used to describe the total number of votes cast, as in 'the share of the vote'.
- The term is occasionally used as an alternative to 'election' ('the vote is on Thursday') and *franchise* ('women have the vote').

vote of confidence: see *no-confidence motion*.

voter: someone who participates by expressing a preference (or casting a *vote*) in an *election* between *candidates* or in a *referendum*. See also *party voter*.

voting behaviour: trends and patterns in groups of *voters* that explain the support in *elections* for particular *candidates* and *political parties*.

wasted votes: a phenomenon, particularly evident under the *first-past-the-post electoral system*, where large numbers of votes do not benefit the *political party* for which they are cast, in terms of contributing to the election of its *candidates*.

- Wasted votes can be either votes cast for the losing candidates in a *constituency* or votes that add to the winning candidate's *majority* (because, to win, a candidate needs only one vote more than the second-placed candidate). It is evident in the results achieved by the Liberal Democrats in the 2001 *general election* when the party won 19% of the votes but only 8% of the *seats*.

- Wasted votes do not feature as prominently under alternative electoral systems where voters rank their preferences on the *ballot papers* (e.g. *alternative vote*) or those that produce *proportional representation* (e.g. *party list*).

- *e.g.* In 2001, the 21,601 votes cast for the Liberal Democrat candidate in the Surrey South West constituency were wasted votes because he came second. In addition, 860 votes cast for the winning Conservative candidate could also be considered as wasted votes, because her majority was 861 when a majority of one vote would have been sufficient to win the seat.

Weatherill Amendment: a *House of Lords amendment* allowing 92 *hereditary peers* to retain their position and voting rights in the Lords when the Labour government's *legislation* of 1999 removed those rights for other hereditary peers.

- The amendment took its name from Lord Weatherill (then leader of the *cross-benchers* in the House of Lords) and was the result of a deal known as the *Cranborne Compromise*.

welfare state: usually described as being created by the 1945 Labour government to provide universal health care, education and social security benefits funded through taxation.

Welsh Assembly (National Assembly for Wales): the devolved *legislature*, based in Cardiff and comprising 60 elected *Members of the Welsh Assembly*, created in 1999 after approval for *devolution* was given by the Welsh *electorate* in a *referendum* in 1997.

- The Welsh Assembly has fewer legislative powers than the devolved *Scottish Parliament*. It cannot, for instance, pass primary *legislation* (which means enabling legislation must be passed by the *Westminster Parliament* granting it authority to pass secondary legislation) or vary the rate of income tax. It has significant administrative powers, however, and, combined with the *Welsh Executive*, it has taken over the functions of the old Welsh Office in *Whitehall*, including responsibility for a budget of £7 billion per annum (e.g. for agriculture, housing and the environment).

Welsh Executive: the devolved *cabinet* with *executive* powers that comprises *Members of the Welsh Assembly* and is presided over by the *first minister* for Wales.

West Lothian question: an anomaly in *representation* resulting from the *devolution* of government from *Westminster*, most famously recognised as a potential problem in the 1970s by Tam Dalyell (the Labour MP for West Lothian).

- What is under question is the imbalance of power created by a *Scottish Parliament* with legislative powers on, for example, education. This means that only *Members of the Scottish Parliament* (and no *representatives* from England) can legislate on Scottish education, whilst all MPs in the Westminster Parliament — including those from Scottish *constituencies* — can vote on *legislation* affecting education in England.

Westminster: the term used interchangeably for *Parliament*, after the area of London where the *House of Commons* and *House of Lords* are located.

Westminster Hall: the alternative debating chamber to the *House of Commons*, also known as the Main Committee, established in 1999.

- All MPs are allowed to attend to discuss, principally, issues raised by *backbenchers* and, occasionally, *select committee* reports. Meetings are held in the Grand Committee Room, off Westminster Hall, on Tuesday and Wednesday mornings and on Thursday afternoons. They are poorly attended and attract little *media* attention.

wets: *Margaret Thatcher's* label for members of the *one-nation conservatism* faction in the *Conservative Party*.

- The wets' opposing faction were adherents to liberal conservatism, and labelled *dries* or *Thatcherites*. Although there were a number of wets in Thatcher's first *cabinet*, she took the opportunity to replace most of these with supporters of her own *ideology* after the 1983 *general election*.
- *e.g.* Sir Ian Gilmour and Sir Francis Pym were prominent wets.

whip: a party manager in *parliament* (in both the *House of Commons* and the *House of Lords*) who works on behalf of the party leadership to ensure *party discipline*, particularly in terms of voting, in the parliamentary party. See *one-line whip*, *two-line whip*, *three-line whip* and *withdrawal of the whip*.

- Whips work as assistants to the *chief whip*. They issue instructions to MPs, arrange *pairing* in the House of Commons and act as a means of communication between the party leadership and *backbenchers*.
- The term also refers to an instruction given to MPs by their party.
- *e.g.* Hilary Armstrong has been Labour's chief whip in the House of Commons since 2001.

whips' office: the collective term for the *chief whips* and assistant *whips*. See also *usual channels*.

Whitehall: a term used interchangeably with *civil service*, after the area of London where most government *department* offices are located.

White Paper: a publication in which the government states its *policy* and announces intended *legislation* on a particular issue.

- A White Paper is regarded as a post-consultative stage in the *legislative process* and may be the subject of a *debate* in the *House of Commons*.
- *e.g.* In 1999, the Labour government published a White Paper, entitled 'Modernising government', on *civil service* reform.

■ *TIP* Be able to distinguish between a White Paper and a *Green Paper*, a consultative document that may come earlier in the legislative process.

winter of discontent: the period of industrial unrest in 1978–79 which is regarded as a contributing factor to the defeat of the Labour government in the 1979 *general election*.

● The *prime minister* at the time, James Callaghan, was criticised for not calling the general election in 1978.

withdrawal of the whip: a punishment (usually temporary) for an MP showing disloyalty, particularly in voting in the *House of Commons*, which effectively means that his or her membership of the parliamentary party is suspended.

■ *e.g.* The most notable recent example occurred in November 1994, when eight *euro-sceptic* Conservative MPs had the whip withdrawn for voting against the government's *bill* to increase the UK's contributions to the *European Union*. The so-called whipless eight were later readmitted to the parliamentary party, thereby restoring the government's *majority*.

women-only shortlists: a device introduced by the *Labour Party* as an attempt to increase the number of female parliamentary *candidates* through rules which insisted that *Constituency Labour Parties* presented a choice of only women to *party members* in their candidate selection process.

● The practice existed between 1993 and 1996 until challenged by two male Labour Party members. An industrial *tribunal* declared these shortlists illegal under the provisions of the Sex Discrimination Act.

Workers' Revolutionary Party: an extreme *left-wing minor party* founded by Gerry Healy, a former *Labour Party* member expelled for being a Trotskyite.

working class: the socioeconomic category of people largely made up of manual workers and their families. See also *class alignment* and *class voting*.

working peer: a member of the *House of Lords* who is nominated by a *political party* to increase its active *representation* in the chamber.

● After the 1997 *general election,* the Labour government appointed a significant number of Labour *life peers* in an attempt to balance the number of Conservative *hereditary peers* and life peers created by Conservative governments between 1979 and 1997.

written constitution: arrangements for government, detailing the composition and responsibilities of the institutions of government and describing their relations, both with each other and with the country's *citizens*, which are written down. See also *unwritten constitution, codified constitution* and *uncodified constitution*.

● The term is often used interchangeably with codified constitution.

■ *e.g.* The USA has a written constitution. The UK's constitution is partially written (in certain *acts of parliament*, for instance) and partially unwritten (in constitutional *conventions*).

written questions: questions put to government *ministers* by MPs for written answers.

- The questions and answers are published in *Hansard*. Written questions are used as a means of scrutinising the government. They are also one of the means by which an MP can seek to redress a *constituent*'s grievances (see also *parliamentary questions*).
- There are approximately 50,000 written questions each year.

X: the mark on a *ballot paper* in an election conducted under the *first-past-the-post* system, whereby a voter indicates a preference for a *candidate* or, in a *referendum*, chooses one of the alternative answers to the question posed.